BUSINESS SUCCESS IN
MENTAL HEALTH PRACTICE

Robert Henley Woody

BUSINESS SUCCESS IN MENTAL HEALTH PRACTICE

Modern Marketing,
Management, and
Legal Strategies

Jossey-Bass Publishers

San Francisco   •   London   •   1989

BUSINESS SUCCESS IN MENTAL HEALTH PRACTICE
Modern Marketing, Management, and Legal Strategies
   by Robert Henley Woody

Copyright © 1989 by: Jossey-Bass Inc., Publishers
                     350 Sansome Street
                     San Francisco, California 94104
                          &
                     Jossey-Bass Limited
                     28 Banner Street
                     London EC1Y 8QE

Library of Congress Cataloging-in-Publication Data

Woody, Robert Henley.
   Business success in mental health practice.

   (The Jossey-Bass social and behavioral science series)
   Bibliography: p.
   Includes index.
   1. Mental health services—Management. I. Title.
II. Series.
RA790.75.W66   1989   362.2'068   89-11046
ISBN 1-55542-168-7 (alk. paper)

Manufactured in the United States of America

The paper in this book meets the guidelines for
permanence and durability of the Committee on
Production Guidelines for Book Longevity of the
Council on Library Resources.

JACKET DESIGN BY WILLI BAUM

FIRST EDITION

Code 8942

THE JOSSEY-BASS
SOCIAL AND BEHAVIORAL SCIENCE SERIES

A CAUTIONARY NOTE

This book is intended to provide accurate and authoritative information in regard to the subject matter. It is sold with the understanding that the publisher and the author are not engaged in rendering legal, accounting, or other professional service. If legal advice or other expert assistance is required, the services of a competent professional, with knowledge of all laws pertaining to the reader, should be sought.

Contents

Preface

TODAY'S MENTAL HEALTH PRACTITIONER IS UNDER tremendous pressure to survive professionally. Diminished governmental funding of mental health services has forced practitioners in ever greater numbers into the private sector. The proliferation of training programs has resulted in, if not a glut on the market, a highly competitive cadre of professionals seeking to attract the same clients. Academic training may impart clinical skills but almost never provides the business skills necessary to succeed in the competitive marketplace. Moreover, professional associations have tended to cling to the antiquated social service model and to resist the modern health-care business model. Thus, with only minimal guidance from training programs or professional associations, mental health practitioners must sink or swim according to their own intuition and initiative.

What This Book Offers

Business Success in Mental Health Practice offers hope for business and professional survival. It contains materials designed to develop skills that are well within the grasp of any mental health practitioner willing and able to open his or her mind to contemporary ideas. This book's contents will be helpful to students, trainees, and veteran practitioners alike. The materials can be used either on an individual basis, for self-improvement, or for classroom instruction. The principles, examples, strategies, and suggestions presented here will be valuable to psychologists in all the clinical specialties, social workers, mental health counselors, marriage and family therapists, sex therapists, physicians, and nurses. The book will be particularly useful to professionals in private practice, but its contents also support the business and financial objectives of public health and social service agencies.

After I had earned doctorates in counseling psychology and health services administration, and after I had gained more than twenty years' experience in mental health services, the "passages" of my life led me to earn a law degree. A lawyer's thought process for analyzing a problem is different from a mental health professional's: The behavioral scientist uses theories and data-based logic and reasoning to explain human behavior, while the lawyer seeks to resolve a reality-oriented conflict by distinguishing the facts unique to a particular legal application; the contrast between concepts and pragmatics is striking. Through legal training, I came to recognize that mental health services are shaped more by social law and the business marketplace than by professional disciplinary preferences. I recognized how training for mental health practice omits certain types of information and cognitions that, if available to trainees, would dramatically improve their personal welfare as well as the contributions they could make to their future clients and to our society.

No matter what their disciplines or how much experience they have, mental health professionals tend to give too little consideration to how public policy governs professionalism. Their training commonly leaves them with deficient knowledge of effective business practices or safeguards against liability. Public policy clearly asserts, however, that mental health services must be conducted with approved business methods, and so success in fulfilling objectives will depend on the use of entrepreneurship.

Mental health practitioners need a well-developed public policy framework for mental health services, in addition to a well-stocked arsenal of strategic weapons (such as marketing techniques) to win the battle for business success. The primary purpose of *Business Success in Mental Health Practice* is to help each reader find the strategies that he or she can adopt and adapt for immediate benefits. Doing so will bring personal rewards, but benefits will also accrue to the profession and to society.

Because of outdated training, the self-serving priorities of professional associations, or personal defensiveness, mental health practitioners all too commonly maintain service-delivery models that ignore contemporary public policy. Such practice creates unnecessary risk of being the subject of an ethical, regulatory, or legal complaint and minimizes opportunities for professional success. Mental health professionals often fail to recognize and accept that mental health services are no longer social services protected by public policy; instead, mental health services are incontrovertibly part of the mammoth health-care industry. As such, they are subject to exacting, business-related demands for accountability, a circumstance reflected by the so-called malpractice crisis.

As a health-care attorney with a background in mental health, I serve mental health practitioners in cases concerning business law, malpractice, professional licensing, and legal consultation. I also regularly conduct professional seminars on entrepreneurship, risk management, and avoiding malpractice in mental health services. Through these activities, I have encountered a host of problems that could have been prevented, and I have met many practitioners who are receiving meager rewards for a great deal of time, effort, and investment. I have also discovered certain solutions to these problems.

In *Business Success in Mental Health Practice,* I share what I have learned about using management, marketing, and the law to achieve success in private practice. In contrast to popular misconceptions of entrepreneurship, I do not define success here solely in terms of money. Success also includes other rewards, such as personal health and happiness, professional respectability, and social contributions. Traditional mental health practitioners are unnecessarily and inappropriately chagrined about pursuing financial payoffs. They seem to believe that setting income as a prominent goal denigrates their professionalism. In today's health-care work, however, professionalism and financial success go hand in hand. Everyone today has financial motives, and in today's health-care world there is certainly no public policy that denies the right to maximize one's income. It is expected, of course, that the consumer will get high-quality service in exchange for payment. Success in mental health practice must be defined by individual priorities, but that determination should be based on information and reality, not on naïveté, insecurity, or misinformation.

This is not a "get rich quick," motivational book—I will leave that arena to others. Its message is "Work hard and do it right, and you will increase your potential for success and rewards." To achieve this educational (or reeducational) objective, I draw on my training in the law, the behavioral sciences, and health services administration and research, as well as on my experiences as a health-care attorney and clinician. The book uses relatively few citations, but every point has the underpinning of academically based knowledge and legal or clinical experience. The mental health professionals for whom I have provided legal services have contributed many of the tried-and-true ideas set forth here; I have helped them, and they have helped me.

I have written two previous books (Woody, 1988a, 1988b) that dealt with minimizing the legal and financial risks of private practice and with avoiding malpractice. In some ways, however, *Business Success in Mental Health Practice* should have been published first. While a mental health practice will always deserve legal and financial protection, and while there should be safeguards against malpractice, many problems can be prevented by a carefully planned, developed, and maintained business system. This book offers the information, with an emphasis on practical suggestions and techniques, for constructing a successful business operation.

Overview of the Contents

Chapter One describes the health-care industry and expenditures for service and explains why a mental health practice is considered a business. Fulfillment of his or her contemporary role and functions justifies and necessitates the practitioner's being entrepreneurial. Entrepreneurship admittedly does reward practitioners, but it also contributes significant benefits to clients and to society. Nevertheless, even though practitioners may support the concept of entrepreneurship, they show strong resistance to marketing. Chapter One defines entrepreneurship and specifies the dimensions or characteristics of successful entrepreneurs.

Chapter Two discusses the purpose and structure of a business plan and points out the link between marketing and business planning. The chapter offers guidance for deciding on a pragmatic mission and defining the services that are to be offered. Chapter Two also presents a thirteen-step approach to business planning, along with ideas about how to use a business plan for a successful mental health practice.

Chapter Three defines marketing and describes how product-oriented marketing is adaptable to service-oriented marketing. The chapter stresses the importance of constructive competition (for example, developing reciprocally beneficial alliances with other mental health practitioners). The chapter also relates marketing to the service-delivery system, with suggestions for market positioning, understanding the current market situation, and conducting a market analysis. Finally, Chapter Three places communication, personalization, selling, and crisis management into a marketing framework and, from the standpoint of ethics, reconciles the differences between public policy and disciplinary preferences.

Chapter Four traces the criticism of professional-services marketing, highlighting changes in governmental regulation and professional ethics. The chapter endorses the integration of modern public policy into professional ethics, defines promotional communication, and compares do-it-yourself promotion with the services provided by advertising agencies. Chapter Four also offers guidance for determining a promotional campaign, allocating financial resources for promotion, selecting promotional strategies, and formulating promotional messages.

Chapter Five describes the selection of professional affiliates and the structural forms of a mental health practice (including sole proprietorship, partnership, and corporation). Much of the material in Chapter Five is also applicable to the selection of a support staff.

Chapter Six offers a conceptualization of the mental health practice as a group and provides ideas for managing group dynamics beneficially. Healthy and unhealthy (pathological) organizational systems are considered, and recommendations are given for remedying destructive conditions.

Chapter Seven deals with the practical matters of selecting, outfitting, and designing an office. It discusses where to locate and how to determine space needs, purchase equipment, and have a functional layout. The chapter also discusses business and risk-management objectives with respect to hiring a support staff, creating teamwork with an accountant and an attorney, managing accounts, keeping essential and legally safe records, managing clients, and managing other professionals.

Chapter Eight defines risk management and describes the nature and effects of ethical, regulatory, legal, and third-party-payer complaints, as well as their negative impacts on emotions, finances, and professional reputation. The chapter's practical risk-management strategies describe how to achieve self-regulation, control associates and staff members, and adopt legally safe policies and practices.

Chapter Nine explains theories and qualities of leadership in a mental health practice group and tells how one can become a chief executive officer (CEO). The emphasis is on retaining professionalism without forfeiting the benefits of entrepreneurship. The chapter also presents two models for a successful mental health CEO.

Chapter Ten underscores the idea that professional success involves more than the number of clients served and dollars earned. It involves achieving a healthy personal, familial, and social life-style. A fulfilling life-style, with health and happiness as goals, is compatible with entrepreneurship and with business success in mental health practice.

Mental health training programs have the responsibility of preparing their trainees for meaningful and constructive engagement in the business world. With this in mind, I have documented and included references for the materials in this book to facilitate their use in the classroom. At the same time, I consistently emphasize pragmatism and make practical suggestions to allow individual professionals, no matter how experienced, to find ideas to improve their practice.

Omaha, Nebraska, and   Robert Henley Woody
Fort Myers, Florida
June 1989

To my wife and professional partner,
Jane Divita Woody,
and to our children,
Matthew, Bob III, and Jennifer

The Author

ROBERT HENLEY WOODY IS A PRACTICING ATTORNEY and psychologist. His law practice is focused on protecting mental health practitioners from ethical, regulatory, and legal complaints. He is a professor of psychology and social work and serves as director of school psychology training at the University of Nebraska, Omaha. He is also an adjunct professor of psychiatry at Michigan State University.

He received his Ph.D. degree in counseling psychology from Michigan State University (1964), his Sc.D. degree in health services administration and research at the University of Pittsburgh (1975), and his J.D. degree from the Creighton University School of Law (1981). During 1966–67, he was a postdoctoral fellow in clinical psychology at the University of London's Institute of Psychiatry (Maudsley Hospital). In 1969, he received the two-year Postdoctoral Certificate in Group Psychotherapy from the Washington School of Psychiatry.

Woody has been admitted by the Nebraska, Michigan, and Florida state bars for the practice of law. He is a licensed psychologist in all three states, as well as a licensed marriage and family therapist in Michigan and Florida. He has been accorded the status of diplomate in clinical psychology by the American Board of Professional Psychology, diplomate in forensic psychology by the American Board of Forensic Psychology, and diplomate in (experimental) psychological hypnosis by the American Board of Psychological Hypnosis. He has been named a fellow of the American Psychological Association, the American Psychological Society, the American Association for Marriage and Family Therapy, the Society for Personality Assessment, the National Academy of Neuropsychologists, and the American Society of Clinical Hypnosis. He is a certified sex therapist and sex educator with the American Association of Sex Educators, Counselors, and Therapists.

Woody has authored or edited twenty-two books and approximately three hundred articles for professional journals. His books include *Counseling Psychology: Strategies and Services* (with J. C. Hansen and R. H. Rossberg, 1989), *Protecting Your Mental Health Practice: How to Minimize Legal and Financial Risk* (1988), *Fifty Ways to Avoid Malpractice: A Guidebook for Mental Health Professionals* (1988), *Becoming a Clinical Psychologist* (with M. Robertson, 1988), *The Law and the Practice of Human Services* (1984), and *The Encyclopedia of Clinical Assessment* (1980).

BUSINESS SUCCESS IN
MENTAL HEALTH PRACTICE

CHAPTER 1

Introduction: Business Realities of Modern-Day Mental Health Practice

AS A HEALTH-CARE ATTORNEY, I FREQUENTLY HEAR comments like these from mental health practitioners: "I'm in a dilemma. I believe that I am well trained for clinical interventions, but I find that there are all sorts of questions that arise for which I have not been prepared to create answers. For one thing, my training emphasized that I was a caregiver and that I should be humanistic in my work with clients. It sounded as though some of my professors thought that I should be unconcerned about getting anything other than an altruistic reward. Almost nothing was taught about how to establish and conduct a mental health practice. I find that good clinical skills are not enough. Some of the ideas that I see in professional newsletters seem to contradict the reality of dealing with clients, who are often quick to complain to ethics committees or licensing boards or even file malpractice suits, and I almost never see a professional association advocating ways to reap financial benefits. I need practical information about how to operate my practice. I've invested a lot of time and money in becoming a professional, and I can't afford to fail. Sometimes I sense that professionalism and modern-day practice are at odds."

This lament is common today among mental health practitioners, whether they are in private practice or public service. Their confusion results from conflicting messages about public preferences for practitioners, on the one hand, and their own professional priorities, on the other. There can be a resolution, however, which will benefit both the public and the professional. The solution involves conceptualizing mental health practice according to contemporary public policy and relying on modern marketing, management, and legal strategies.

Over a century ago, technology ushered in the industrial revolution. An industrial leader could gain personal satisfaction, social prominence, and wealth by being in the right place at the right time and conducting business wisely. The contemporary mental health professional has a similar opportunity. This is the dawning of a revolution in mental health care. A mental health professional can now gain personal satisfaction, social prominence, and wealth by adopting a sound business approach to mental health services.

Mental Health as a Business

Unfortunately, professional training programs seldom if ever provide emerging professionals with the knowledge and skills necessary for successful business operations. Moreover, seasoned practitioners are often fettered by their professional associations' self-serving pursuits—for example, the institutionalization of disciplinary role definitions, as reflected in codes of professional ethics or endorsed service-delivery guidelines. These barriers to success can be overcome, however, and this book is designed to prepare mental health practitioners to honor their disciplinary ethics and standards while progressing beyond their training limitations and obtaining the knowledge and skills necessary to compete successfully in today's complex health-care industry.

The threshold issue is to conceptualize mental health practice as a business. Training programs are infamous for their idealism. Teaching faculty members seldom effectively bridge the gap between theory and practice. More often than not, trainers have little or no experience with "fighting in the trenches." A faculty member who does engage in, say, private clinical practice is apt to encounter faculty colleagues who believe that promotion, tenure, and salary increases should be delayed or withheld because of this "outside activity." Rarely is such a person applauded for "staying in the front lines" and bringing the reality and richness of clinical practice to the classroom. The outcome, of course, is that students and trainees are deprived of preparation for what they will actually confront—a demanding, business-oriented scene. In other words, new professionals are too often led to accept a faulty conceptualization of contemporary mental health services.

To be sure, there was an era, not so long ago, when mental health services were correctly conceptualized as existing within a nonbusiness framework. From the nineteenth-century almshouses to the twentieth-century community mental health movement, public policy supported the idea that mental health professionals should be altruistic and nurturant. Their salaries were modest, but they received social recognition for their benevolent efforts. Mental health professionals were also granted distinct protection from certain kinds of social assaults. For example, the concept of charitable immunity protected them from lawsuits, and any complaint from a client was essentially processed by a disciplinary ethics committee, which seldom did more than give the errant practitioner a slap on the wrist.

Today is another era. Mental health services are now seen as part of the mammoth health-care industry. Professional incomes have skyrocketed and will probably continue to increase, notwithstanding the increased availability of health care generally and the greater market competition among professionals (Parsons, Youkstetter, Burton, and Willson, 1986).

Society has also removed the protective cloak: All forms of immunity have been eroded, and a malpractice crisis now exists (Woody, 1988a). Disciplinary ethics committees are virtually ignored, and their remaining assignments focus on education and referral (American Psychological Association, 1987b). The old boys'/old girls' clubs cultivated by professional disciplines have been replaced by the judicial process.

Health-Care Expenditures

Society has become very conscious of quality-of-life issues and is demanding more and more health-related services. According to Barnes (1986, p. 40), "In 1978, $600 billion or 45% of the average family's budget was spent on services. Despite the obvious importance of service marketing, only recently have academic marketers turned their attention to this realm of activity." It is estimated that by the 1990s, the average expenditure will be over 50 percent and that "services will account for more than half of the nation's economic activity by the end of the 1980s" (Webster, 1987, pp. 12–13).

The expectations for health care are also increasing. While the prevailing view may be that costs should be minimized but service should be maximized (Mechanic, 1981), public policy pushes for more and better health care, and expenditures reflect a growth industry: "As demand for health care services increased, the industry has mushroomed. Health care has gone from 5.8% of the Gross National Product (GNP) in 1960 to 10.7% in 1984" (Parker, 1987, pp. 11–12). According to Spitz and Sauber (1987, pp. 119–120), "National health expenditure increased substantively in the past 26 years (from $12.7 billion in 1950 to $365 billion in 1984)," and they provide details: "National expenditures for 1982 were approximately $322.4 [billion] .... Of this total expended for health care, the private sector spent $185.6 billion, the federal sector spent $93.2 billion, while state and local government sectors spent $43.7 billion. Projections for 1990 are that total expenditures will surpass $490 billion. Of this the private sector will spend approximately $211 billion while state and local government sectors will spend about $82 [billion] ...." In view of these mind-boggling amounts, it is clear that our society wants health care and is willing to pay for it.

Given the diversity of payment sources and types of service providers, it is difficult to estimate with reasonable exactitude the amount of money spent for mental health services. Suffice it to say that analyses of expenditures for health care in general always include mental health care as a specific, and the annual amount is huge (Saywell and McHugh, 1986). For example, consider Kiesler and Sibulkin's (1987, p. 21) report on Medicare: "The federally funded health insurance program for the aged and disabled spent $995 million on mental health care in 1981, and over 80% was for inpatient care." They identify 1977 expenditures of $587 million for Medicaid-sponsored mental health programs. Adding other payment sources, they conclude that "a total figure of approximately $1 billion was spent in FY 77 on mental hospitalization through Medicaid" (p. 22).

There are other sources for payment for mental health services, such as out-of-pocket payments by the client or third-party payments by health insurance companies. Another reality is that health insurance has become a vital necessity for most people: "Health insurance has come to be considered a requirement by most Americans. Prior to 1940, fewer than 10% of Americans had health insurance coverage. Now more than 80% of the population is covered" (Parker, 1987, p. 12). Given the integral role of mental health in people's lives and the magnitude of the financial expenditure, it is not surprising that public policy has stripped away disciplinary control of mental health services in favor of governmental regulation (such as by state agencies and the judicial system).

Professional Restrictions on the Marketing of Services

Earlier, I mentioned the hesitancy until now of academic marketers to study the marketing of professional services (see Barnes, 1986, p. 40). Usually marketers are quick to plunge into uncharted waters; to do otherwise would be a contradiction of the exploratory or promotional nature of marketing. In the case of professional services, however, there has been an endemic resistance to marketing on the part of providers. Mental health practitioners, in fact, seem to constitute one of the more defensive sectors of health-care services.

The notion of professionalism has unwisely been allowed to constitute a barrier to the aggressive promotion of one's mental health practice. Mahon (1978) states: "Sometimes the philosophical background of one's profession is permitted to get in the way and unnecessarily inhibit efforts to expand the practice. This can be a serious psychological deterrent. All the professions, especially the learned ones, have long disavowed profits as a principal objective. Each has professed a loftier purpose or ideal—a philosophical obligation to apply its knowledge and experience toward improving mankind's condition in a spirit of genuine service. This ideal has been drilled into students in all the professions" (p. 30). Mahon, while pointing out that traditional philosophical precepts continue to influence the standards for professional service, believes that there need be no conflict between service and financial motives: "Actually, there is no fundamental conflict between the desirability of maintaining a professional image on the one hand and the need to take appropriate steps to enlarge one's practice on the other. It is only necessary that the steps be appropriate, tasteful, and in harmony with the profession's traditional dignity and image. Indeed, far from hindering growth efforts, the professional aura, when delicately exploited, can be the single most important element in marketing services" (p. 4).

Mahon's message is insightful and accurate, but public policy has moved away from requiring that a practitioner's promotional efforts "be appropriate, tasteful, and in harmony with the profession's traditional dignity and image," favoring instead full disclosure (truthful and not misleading) to enhance quality and competitive pricing. For example, the Federal Trade Commission has demanded that the American Psychological Association abolish its ethical principles that prohibit fee splitting and some kinds of advertising (Bales, 1988). (More will be said on this matter later, in discussions of marketing and advertising.)

Social Benefits of Marketing

An important point is that the promotion of professional services, such as through marketing strategies, creates a benefit for society. This benefit can be succinctly referred to as *health promotion*. Health-care practitioners are quick to applaud public education that promotes healthful behavior. The marketing of professional health care leads to greater awareness of health in the public mind and to greater availability of services.

Marketing produces a benefit for the public, but it is the proverbial double-edged sword for professionals. It produces competition among service providers: Some will get ahead, and some will fall behind. Marketing also wrests control of service delivery from professional associations and vests it with regulatory agencies.

Resistance to Marketing

It would be admirable if professional associations' efforts to regulate their members were exclusively or even primarily for the public good, but that is not true. In fact, a professional association is an institution, and an institution by its very nature is at least partly devoted to perpetuating its own existence, even at the expense of its members or others. Where mental health associations are concerned, the public has become suspicious of activities that seem to benefit the discipline (and thus the association) more than they help society or consumers of mental health services. Consequently, numerous legal confrontations have found guardians of the public interest on one side and professional associations on the other. The outcome of these clashes has been a definite weakening of the associations' control over disciplines. For example, antitrust laws now prohibit monopolistic efforts by a professional association, such as efforts that would limit professional advertising (Overcast, Sales, and Pollard, 1982).

To this day, professionals who would like to market their services are reluctant to do so for fear of violating ethical codes. What should be recognized is that a code of ethics must benefit consumers, professionalism is not a preordained or permanent right, and professional ethics have evolved and are still changing. Clients' expectations have also changed, and services are selected for their quality and not because of mere "awe of the professional's credentials" (Webster, 1987, p. 12). It is dissonant with public policy for professionals to disdain commercialism or to equate the marketing of professional services with the crass selling of a product. Likewise, by public policy and law, professional associations cannot promulgate ethical or service-delivery restrictions that do not benefit consumers or society.

Although this fact is perhaps unknown to or unacknowledged by their members, professional associations have wisely (although, perhaps, reluctantly) moved forward with the changing dictates of public policy. For example, they have removed their unjustified restrictions on marketing and advertising. Unfortunately, however, individual practitioners are often poorly informed or ill advised about the contemporary ethics or service-delivery guidelines of their own professional associations or about statutes for and rules from relevant licensing boards.

There is a distinct tendency for mental health professionals to remain bonded to the ethics or standards that existed during their primary training. Even if a professional is exposed to a modern position statement, he or she may discount it and fail to absorb it. Similarly inclined and misinformed colleagues, of whom some end up on ethics committees, may wrongly advise practitioners in accord with outdated notions. These circumstances not only are liable to lead to unsuccessful practice but also invite the filing of complaints against practitioners with ethics committees, state regulatory agencies, or courts of law.

Given these changes in public policy, the increase in practitioners' legal liability, and the surge in competition among mental health disciplines and among colleagues within a discipline, the prudent mental health professional must forsake outmoded notions about the "protections" accorded to social service and accept that mental health is a business, and that one's clinical practice must be operated accordingly. This approach will require astute management of all resources, business analysis and planning, and aggressive marketing (including diverse promotional and advertising methods). One must also adopt a systematic approach to management, one that encompasses efficiency, effectiveness, and legal safeguards. What is most fundamental is that the mental health professional must be able to manifest entrepreneurial qualities. (Entrepreneurship, of course, must still exist within the guidelines of current professional ethics, and the reader is advised to stay well informed about them.

Since ethics are now, perhaps more than ever, undergoing change, constant vigilance is required.)

The Structure of Entrepreneurship

Entrepreneurship is neither taught nor encouraged in the typical mental health training program. If anything, it is contradicted and discouraged. As we have seen, this is a disservice to the budding professional and to society. Where such a deficiency exists, it should be viewed as a shortcoming of the program and its professors.

The Prerequisite Dimension. There was a time when entrepreneurship depended largely on family wealth. The success or failure of an entrepreneurial effort could be predicted on the basis of family contacts and status in the community. Times have changed, however. According to Casson (1982, p. 387), "Educational qualifications are very important in reducing the constraints imposed by personal wealth. Not only do they give entry to establishment institutions, they are also used as a screening device in recruiting managers. One way or another, therefore, they regulate the entrepreneur's access to other people's capital."

In the realm of professional services, the necessary and right educational qualifications are the prerequisites for entrepreneurial success. Nevertheless, some educational qualifications may be met or supplemented by instruction received in the school of hard knocks. Professional and educational qualifications may be necessary for getting a license to practice and will be helpful for justifying fees and gaining financial support (such as a business loan). Beyond a certain point, however, they cease to give the impetus one needs for entrepreneurial success.

The Investment Dimension. This exploration of the meaning of entrepreneurship starts with the fact that the mental health professional has made an incalculable investment in his or her career. Basically, the practitioner's life has been devoted to the profession, and it will determine the life-style and the opportunities of the practitioner and all members of his or her family. The practitioner's degree of personal satisfaction will profoundly affect his or her personality, relationships, health, and perhaps longevity. Any financial gain will provide for necessities, such as a house, transportation, education, health services, and so on. On a mundane level, the professional has taken financial resources that he or she could have used otherwise (say, for "adult toys") and spent the money on training. He or she has also taken priceless time away from personal and family pleasure and spent it in the classroom.

The Financial Dimension. It is nothing short of amazing that a well-trained professional, after spending thousands of dollars on career preparation and hundreds of hours on professional training, can feel guilty about collecting fees for service (as is justified by the prevailing health-care marketplace). Nevertheless, unsuccessful mental health professionals often rationalize their meager incomes by self-created notions of having to function individually as public social service agencies. If our society wants public social services, it will fund them. The financial recalcitrant is revealing a character flaw, a personal insecurity.

Under contemporary public policy, the logical mental health professional need not apologize for giving high priority to the goal of financial gain, nor need he or she feel guilty over the fee required to buy his or her professional services. The service recipient has no entitlement until there is the creation and maintenance of a value-for-value exchange: The professional has a duty to provide high-quality service to the client who pays for it, but this duty does not automatically extend to others who have not made such payment.

Benevolence may lead one to offer free service on some occasions, but those should be purposeful exceptions. Otherwise, recipients must pay to justify their receipt of services. The practitioner may make a purposeful contribution, but he or she has no reason to routinely feel sorry for clients who cannot afford services. Moreover, the failure to adhere to a standardized system for charging and collecting fees portends elevated risk of a complaint or legal action—the greater his or her debt, the more apt a client is to file a complaint when an effort is made to collect the money owed (Woody, 1988b). Instead of allowing his or her fee to be an occasion for neurotic guilt or unproductive sympathy for the downtrodden, the professional should consider making a commitment of time and effort to try to shape and change public policy in a manner that will lead our society to better meet the needs of the disenfranchised—and there is great room for improvement in our social welfare system.

The Social Benefit Dimension. Entrepreneurship involves more than income or profit. It is a quest to benefit the practitioner personally and society generally: "An important feature of being entrepreneurial is that you provide something of value to others. The greater the need people have for your product or service, the greater your rewards will be. If you work to help other people to raise their standards of living and to improve their lives, you will be serving the needs of society. This is the meaning of being an entrepreneur" (Meredith, Nelson, and Neck, 1982, p. 7). Schollhammer and Kuriloff (1979) concur: "They [entrepreneurs] provide economic good in the form of product or service; income for those who work for them; a share in the profits of the operation for their shareholders; and, when they manage well, continuity of existence ensuring their ability to make these contributions over the years" (p. 25). From this stance, the mental health practitioner can find the coveted social service reward. After all, if psychotherapy is successfully marketed, more clients will receive the service and improve their lives, and society will be strengthened.

The Scientist-Practitioner Dimension. Throughout history, as during the industrial revolution, entrepreneurs have been "moved by a burning interest in applying findings of science and in gaining massive increases in productive output through the use of new technology" (Schollhammer and Kuriloff, 1979, p. 8). It is in keeping with mental health professionalism to have a dedication to advancing and applying science in order to increase productivity—for example, making therapeutic innovations available to a greater number of service recipients or clients. Risk management does not allow for foolhardy experimentation; even innovation must be predicated on an academic rationale. In malpractice suits, negligence is determined according to a reasonable standard of care, which is defined by an appropriate blending of scientific knowledge and considerations of practice. Public policy has declared that mental health professionals have a responsibility to further the scientific understanding of human behavior and to remedy mental and behavioral problems. Fulfillment of this responsibility is rewarded with entrepreneurial benefits.

The Personal Dimension. Given theories and research on career development, it seems indisputable to assert that a person's career is, to a large extent, determined by his or her need fulfillment. Entrepreneurship does fulfill needs. For example, McClelland's (1967) research supports the idea that entrepreneurs have a strong need for achievement and are stimulated by feedback; their second most important need is for proof of competence, which is documented by financial gain, among other things. Since all career choices involve personal need fulfillment, there is nothing negative about entrepreneurial need fulfillment.

Certain traits are aligned with entrepreneurship. Foremost, perhaps, is the ability to take risks: "Entrepreneurs are calculated risk-takers. They enjoy the excitement of a challenge, but they don't gamble. Entrepreneurs avoid low-risk situations because there is a lack of challenge and avoid high-risk situations because they want to succeed. They like *achieveable* challenges" (Meredith, Nelson, and Neck, 1982, p. 25). This idea is in accord with McClelland's (1967) view that entrepreneurs prefer moderate risks. Risk taking requires creativity and innovation, which turn ideas into reality. Realism restricts activities to situations in which the entrepreneur can affect outcomes. As a group, mental health practitioners are not prone to risk taking, but its presence does often distinguish those practitioners who enjoy notable success from those who fail to reap the potential harvests of their profession.

There are other, related, traits that identify entrepreneurs. Self-confidence and a realistic knowledge of capabilities

(Merdedith, Nelson, and Neck, 1982) combined with a desire for responsibility, a high energy level, and a futuristic orientation (McClelland, 1967) portray the entrepreneur. Schollhammer and Kuriloff (1979) believe that entrepreneurs are self-starters and are able to get things done, qualities crucial to organizing for success. They also believe that a person's entrepreneurial potential depends on his or her innovative ability, tolerance for ambiguity, desire to achieve, realistic planning ability, goal-oriented leadership, objectivity, personal responsibility (the locus of control should be internal), adaptability, and ability to organize and administer. Meredith, Nelson, and Neck (1982) offer a similar catalogue: self-confidence (with individuality and optimism), task-result orientation (with need for achievement, profit orientation, persistence, perseverance, determination, energy), risk taking (with enjoyment of challenges), leadership (with adaptability and responsiveness to others, ability to take suggestions and criticisms), originality (with innovation, creativity, flexibility, open-mindedness, resourcefulness, versatility, knowledgeability), and future orientation (with foresight and perceptiveness).

Entrepreneurship is a developmental, personal quality. It can afford self-actualization. Entrepreneurs "find dignity and worth in their work, but most rewarding is the self-fulfillment that the work makes possible, the doing of a hard job well" (Schollhammer and Kuriloff, 1979, p. 25). Entrepreneurs also experience a coveted feeling of independence: "They are their own persons in a psychological sense, and this trait gives them a feeling of freedom, of lack of constraints, that they value" (Schollhammer and Kuriloff, 1979, p. 25).

As with any self-understanding effort, the mental health practitioner should engage in a self-evaluation that compares his or her current situation with the desired goal. (Chapter Two will provide an analysis of the system that can lead to improved entrepreneurial goals.)

The Operational Dimension. The entrepreneur constantly evaluates, with the objective of being more successful. According to Meredith, Nelson, and Neck (1982, p. 3), "Entrepreneurs are

people who have the ability to see and evaluate business opportunities; to gather the necessary resources to take advantage of
them; and to initiate appropriate action to ensure success." It is
difficult to believe that any mental health professional would
dispute the desirability of such an operational framework.

The tasks performed by the entrepreneur are quite varied.
Baty (1981, p. 178) proposes that there is a continuum of tasks
ranging from those of the "pure entrepreneur" to those of the
"pure custodian," and that every professional may do a bit of
entrepreneurship and a bit of custodianship: "Roughly defined,
the entrepreneurial tasks involve the *setting up, planning,* and
motivational activities of the firm. They would include such
things as initiating market research, recruiting a banker, an accountant, an ad agency, finding a building, setting budgets, and
so on. The custodial tasks, by contrast, are such things as track-
ing budgets, developing financial reports, purchasing materials,
supervising production, refereeing disputes between production
and marketing. Entrepreneurial tasks are much less delegable as
a rule than are custodial tasks" (emphasis in original). The goal
for the professional is to eliminate as many custodial tasks as
possible, without losing operational control or increasing costs.

Keeping control is a major objective for the entrepreneur.
When forming practice groups, mental health practitioners are
apt to think that all members are created equal. This kind of
thinking is not part of the business model. Chapter Nine will
deal with being a chief executive officer, and Chapter Five will
cover the group dynamics that should be cultivated in a mental
health practice. For now, it is sufficient to say that the entrepreneur does not allow a pressing immediate need ("Let's form a
practice group") automatically to overpower long-range goals
("I want to maximize my benefits"). A judgment about making
someone a partner rather than an employee is a control issue
and should be based on long-range objectives. The entrepreneur
realizes that it is shortsighted to take on a partner merely to
have a seemingly balanced team or to impress financial backers,
unless that partner will make a lifelong, substantial contribution
to the development and maintenance of the operation. Baty
(1981) suggests that no tentative offer be extended to a poten-

tial partner until the entrepreneur has progressed as far as possible without the other person's assistance, and that if it is possible to hire an employee, it may be unwise to accept a partner, who will forever share in the profits.

The Mental Health Composite. The personal characteristics necessary for entrepreneurship do not contradict those needed for facilitating mental health interventions. As can be discerned quickly, entrepreneurial qualities have a logical connection to any pursuit of excellence, regardless of discipline or objective. Nevertheless, certain forces may wrongly divert the mental health practitioner from the entrepreneurial route—for example, arrangements that allow a professional association to maintain inappropriate control over the practitioner. After all, an entrepreneur is committed to learned judgments and self-determination and would resist allowing an external entity any preordained or irrevocable control over his or her endeavors. The nature of clinical practice also involves a long-range plan and a stable (almost fixed) routine (seeing clients every hour on the hour, day after day). This structure may impose a stance against risk taking. With this structure, there is minimal flexibility, and the strength of the practice is slowly built while setbacks are avoided. Certainly, everyone wants to avoid career setbacks, but entrepreneurship requires at least a modicum of *calculated* risk taking, and this may be one of the most difficult things for the would-be mental health entrepreneur to do.

Conclusions

The foregoing material constructs a rationale for entrepreneurship as the foundation of contemporary mental health practice. Professional training programs have failed so far to equip practitioners for the realities of belonging to the health-care industry. Nevertheless, society is unrelenting in its desire for accountability in the professions and expects mental health practices to be conducted in a businesslike manner. If mental health professionals do not meet society's expectations, they will suffer economic and legal sanctions. Professional associations do seem to be recognizing the shift toward a business model, but many practitioners are clinging unnecessarily and unwisely to the past. In the process, they are courting financial penalties and an elevated risk of complaints to ethical, regulatory, and legal bodies.

No logic excuses a mental health professional's failure to operate a practice according to business principles, and to do otherwise is to demonstrate one's incompetence and poor judgment. The practitioner has invested heavily in becoming a professional, and dividends depend on entrepreneurship. The mental health entrepreneur is not totally egocentric and does not quest blindly after the almighty dollar. On the contrary, he or she recognizes, accepts, and maximizes our society's espoused roles and duties of a mental health practitioner. The benefits of a successful practice extend also to service recipients, clients, and society. In fact, nonentrepreneurial practice can deprive society of the benefits it sought in the first place by endorsing professional services.

CHAPTER 2

Planning for Business

THE MOVEMENT OF MENTAL HEALTH SERVICES FROM being predominantly a social service to being part of the business world does not lessen its dedication to high-quality care. It only reveals a newfound commitment to business success. Entrepreneurship principles determine whether a mental health practice will be adequate at best or highly successful. Entrepreneurial leadership is essential to success. Leadership requires the mental health practitioner to adopt the stance of a chief executive officer or chief executive for operations (CEO) and to deal with associates in a way that will keep the tenets of better business in the forefront. This same thrust is inherent in the management of everyone involved in the practice, professionals (partners or associates) and laypersons (support staffers) alike. From this stance, the mental health CEO should lead the practice group to systematic business planning.

The Purpose of a Business Plan

A business plan is essential to the functioning of the entire mental health practice: "Strategic management is an ongoing process which includes long-range plans, medium-range plans, and daily or operational plans" (Forman and Forman, 1987, p. 28). No matter how sage or experienced the practitioner may be, operating without the benefit of a formally conceived business plan is more likely than not to impede success.

17

The business plan provides a central and detailed statement about what the mental health practice will do and how it will accomplish it. It is more, however, than simply setting forth what services will be offered ("Psychotherapy for adults, no services for children or adolescents").

The Structure of the Business Plan

When hearing about a specific strategy or method, such as business planning, the mental health professional is prone to ask, "Where can I find a model business plan to which I can plug in my information?" As with most other documents for mental health practice, it is possible to glean information from a sample document, but it is unwise to try to adopt one.

The whole nature of a planning document is directed at assessing needs, potentials, resources, and goals unique to the practice. In other words, the form, structure, and contents of the business plan are determined by the intended makeup and use of the particular practice: As a result, "the form of documentation, the emphasis, the depth of background support, the statistical bounding (best/worst/expected), the line-item detail of financial projections, the sampling rate (weekly, monthly, or yearly) of projections, and other features may vary according to intended use" (Baty, 1981, p. 89). Regardless of the form, business planning "enables the user to gather relevant data about a firm's operations, make forecasts and predictions, clarify goals, establish goal-directed actions, identify mechanisms for future data collection, and check the results that will be used to correct errors" (Forman and Forman, 1987, p. 28).

Regarding the business plan, the mental health business can best accomplish its goals by a systemic design, such as by using innovation in service delivery and marketing, projections of costs, and so on (Cunningham and Bennett, 1987). The systemic approach to business planning should accommodate seven dimensions (Mahon, 1978). In business planning, these dimensions are interrelated and must be recognized and shaped by their reciprocal forces.

1. A strong and efficient organization (for example, with pragmatic administration and management)
2. Adequate geographical coverage for the services (for example, having an adequate population base from which to draw clients)
3. A complete product or service line (for example, having adequate diversity of mental health services to ensure business)
4. Technical competence and quality (for example, employing professionals who are capable of offering comprehensive care)
5. Special competence (for example, employing professionals with up-to-date skills for critical needs of clients)
6. Competitive fees (for example, establishing financial policies that honor competence, quality, and the marketplace)
7. Dedication to service (for example, a commitment to hard work to advance the practice in accord with the standards of the profession)

Marketing and Business Planning

Marketing provides critical dimensions for the business plan, and the marketing objective is interwoven throughout all business planning. Unless its mental health services are successfully marketed, the practice will fail. Advertising is only one part of marketing in general, but it can serve as a micro example of how macro business planning and marketing are related. Part of establishing a good advertising plan is to use situational analysis (which will be described in Chapter Three). By dissecting the strengths, weaknesses, and objectives of the mental health practice, understanding the service characteristics and the available clientele, and drawing on insights about the other mental health practitioners in the community, the mental health CEO can use situational analysis to construct an effective advertising campaign (Ray, 1982). When there is no awareness of marketing, a business plan is esoteric and impractical. Therefore, as business planning is explored, the marketing backdrop should always be acknowledged and a systemic analysis should be applied to all business-related dimensions.

Mental health professionals often have difficulty accepting the idea that marketing their services is more similar to than different from product marketing. In business planning, the compatibility is striking; the processes are quite similar, whether the objective is to sell a product or attract clients who need clinical services. A necessary part of business planning for mental health services is to be mindful of the goal of selling the service.

Deciding on a Mission

The business plan is intended to move the organization toward attainment of its mission, and the mission in turn reflects the marketing objective. The term *mission* should not be seen as a mere pretension. The mission embodies one's purpose for being in business as a mental health practitioner. It is naïve to state "helping others" as one's mission. To be sure, every mental health practitioner must be dedicated to helping others, but in the context of business planning, the mission defines the unique goals espoused by the organization and its personnel, as well as the means of achieving them. For example, a behavioral practice might pursue a mission of "providing professional expertise for the application of behavioral science and learning-based strategies for the modification of maladaptive behavior responses, and of doing so with efficacy and economy."

A major challenge is to settle on what services to provide. Regardless of his or her discipline or level of training, every mental health practitioner has multiple skills and can fulfill various clients' needs.

For at least three reasons, it is unwise to try to be all things to all people. First, the practitioner will probably find the demands too taxing. Up to a point, diversification can be stimulating, and change can motivate, but having to meet expectations that exceed his or her competence may cause the sensitive practitioner to feel pressed into gaining new skills. While new skills are desirable, however, good performance and maximum productivity demand that inner strengths and resources not be squandered. Prudent use of resources requires that a realistic field of service be chosen.

Second, the practitioner will probably find that offering a wide variety of services has negative connotations for potential clients. It is egocentric to believe that proclaiming one's every skill or possible type of service will impress clients and capture their patronage. On the contrary, clients sometimes interpret a profusion of skills and services as suggesting a desperation for business. Effective marketing calls for a reasonable narrowing down of skills and services. Success may come more readily from being one of the best at a few things and for a few people.

Third, the practitioner must meet the standard of care for every special skill or service offered to clients. In fact, the practitioner does not even have to state the skill or service explicitly to be held to the specialized standard. If a reasonable client could infer from a brochure or an advertisement that a practitioner is a specialist in a particular service, then a regulatory or malpractice action against the practitioner would probably rely on the highest possible standard of care. Thus, risk management is a good reason to delimit one's skills and services and restrict the types of clients one accepts for treatment.

Defining the Services

Mental health professionals often assume that everyone understands clinical services. It is true that our society has moved a long way toward accepting the idea that everyone probably can benefit from mental health services, but there is still much misunderstanding about mental health services and practitioners. For example, confusion is common about the distinctions among psychiatrists, psychologists, social workers, and mental health counselors.

To use business planning effectively, not to mention the marketing objective, it is essential to define what services are going to be offered. (Of course, the services offered may change from time to time, according to needs in the marketplace and the resources of the mental health organization.) Risk management, too, is furthered by the defining of skills and services in the business plan. Risk management is more than avoiding malpractice. Another of its major purposes is to safeguard and maximize financial and other resources. By defining skills and services, the mental health CEO will know in which basket to put the eggs. If there is accurate understanding of which skills and services should be given business support, it will be easier to avoid accepting poor-risk clients, assigning personnel counterproductively, and incurring unjustified financial obligations.

Approaching Business Planning

Many varieties of possible business plans exist, and the selection of a planning approach must be based on the needs and characteristics of the particular mental health practice. In general, the business planning processes should do the following (Forman and Forman, 1987):

- Set long-range objectives and short-range goals
- Posit strategies for achieving the objectives and goals
- Create a mission-related philosophy to produce an organizational climate
- Develop operational and risk-management policies
- Devise an organizational structure with specified functions, including recruiting, selecting, hiring, training, paying, and terminating personnel
- Establish management (including communication) procedures
- Answer questions pertaining to physical location, facility, and materials procurement and management
- Secure necessary capital and arrange for contingency financing
- Prescribe standards for service
- Establish management programs and operational plans
- Determine the choice of an information-management system
- Set forth a scheme for activating, motivating, and directing employees for the benefit of the business enterprise.

Since this is still a planning stage, however, none of these decisions is irrevocable. All decisions should be evaluated and possibly modified.

Based on a well-established product model for business planning (Baty, 1981), the following contemporary mental health service model for business planning contains thirteen steps for the mental health CEO to consider. While these are somewhat progressive, which means that they probably should be used in the sequence presented, there are always exceptions. For example, step 3 may or may not precede step 4. There can also be a "hopscotching over the steps." For example, step 1 will necessarily draw bits of information from all or most of the later steps, perhaps even the last one. Nevertheless, each successive step must be refined according to the preceding steps. The entire model relies on unification and integration of the steps. Reference will be made to the role of the mental health CEO. He or she will rely on a team approach of shared responsibility. Technically, the analytical data for each step should be reduced to a written statement, with the components formulating an overall planning document.

Step 1: The Miniplan. The CEO considers everything that will probably be needed to accomplish the chosen objectives. Consideration is also given to systemic effects of the interacting factors. From this preliminary analysis, a summary of the essential facts (with at least some consideration of possible but "unproved" facts) is prepared.

Step 2: Background of the Plan. In this step, the CEO describes the origins of the clinical services. Business opportunities are identified and realistically assessed according to the resources of the practice, the characteristics of the community, and the CEO's preferred clientele.

Step 3: The Team. The CEO describes each professional and support staff person. This step contains a number of implications for risk management (see Chapter Eight). At the planning stage, the describing of individual qualifications allows recognition and appreciation of strengths and weaknesses and allows modification or tailoring of later steps. At this point, it is also a good idea to prepare an organizational chart that depicts duties, responsibilities, and communication channels (management authority—who will direct what—deserves special attention).

Step 4: Service Description. This is described in more detail in Chapters Three and Four. For now, the service description will state what the mental health practice will and will not do. This is a defining and delimiting exercise. With objectivity, the service description should say why the practice and its professionals are superior to the competition, such as other mental health practices in the immediate community that provide similar services and draw from the same client population (or market section). Part of this appraisal of the competition will involve specifying what benefits clients of the practice will gain, with the implication that they would not gain the same or as many benefits from another mental health practice.

Step 5: Ownership. This step provides a legal framework for financing and governance in the present or in the future. Other rights and duties are also formalized, such as stock options (if any) and additional financial and management commitments. Much of this step is determined by the already established form of business entity that has been accepted for the mental health practice.

Step 6: The Market. Here, the CEO presents documented evidence of market growth, trends in fees (or prices), and need(s) for service. Given the many types of mental health service providers and the confidential nature of clinical services, it is difficult to locate objective data on these trends, for the reliability and validity of survey-based data on these matters must always be treated as suspect. The prudent mental health CEO will be on guard against relying too much on any one source, no matter how prestigious or authoritative it may appear to be. Among other things, this analytical description may include calculations based on experience with past and current clients, as well as a qualitative listing of established and potential referral sources.

All possible interpretive assumptions should be made at this point.

Step 7: Marketing Strategy. This step is unsurpassed in its importance for determining business success. It must be prominent early in planning and throughout the operation of the mental health practice. For now, the business plan should include detailed ideas about sales, promotion, and delivery. Tentative schedules and costs should be determined, and critical events should be anticipated.

Step 8: The Operation. This step describes the operation of the mental health business. Planning should consider how the business will operate; the CEO can prepare learning curves and lists of vendors. (The term *vendors* refers to ancillary professionals who can provide specialized supervision or unusual clinical services and to others who can assist the operations of the practice, such as accountants or attorneys with special competence in mental health practice.) As much as possible, the timing of decisions should be established, such as when certain changes will be made in the practice (including the addition of professional or support personnel, equipment purchases, or expansion). The facilities must always be suitable, and care should be exercised to eliminate unnecessary barriers. For example, the CEO should avoid signing a lease for office space if the lease would prohibit expansion or require payments that strained the budget (watch out for an annual increase based on a national financial index, or for a tenant's assumption of property tax in this roller-coaster tax era). A decision on how to operate should include a predictable inventory, such as the substantial cost associated with having a well-stocked supply of psychological tests, biofeedback equipment, and so on.

Step 9: Research and Development. Being academically oriented, mental health professionals should have no difficulty accepting the need for research and development to maintain and improve their practices. Unfortunately, however, these professionals are in no way immune to the human foibles of being rigid or having closed minds, and so they often stint on expenditures of time or money for research and development. Nevertheless, entrepreneurship in general demands a continued search for the proverbial better mousetrap, and this principle is no less applicable to mental health services. The mental health business plan should give consideration to how research and development can complement objectives, costs, and schedules and enhance service delivery and risk management.

Step 10: Staffing. This step expands step 3. While in step 3 the team is defined by personnel and their qualifications, in this step staffing determines timetables (flowcharts are useful) and the skills needed for optimal productivity and service. Such planning must not ignore concerns for availability and costs, yet one must still be willing to invest capital to accomplish the goals of entrepreneurship. In other words, this step will reveal any gaps in resources and may prompt greater expenditures. The end goal, of course, is efficiency of function, efficacy of operation, and profit.

Step 11: The Financial Strategy. Step 11 will tell the story of the success or the failure of the entire mental health business venture. Because they lack training in this area, mental health professionals tend to be naïve about financial issues. Consequently, they must be willing and able to bring in consultants who have special expertise. A skilled financial analyst can accomplish many tasks, including those related to the assessment of financial ratios, sources and uses of funds, break-even analysis and operating leverage, bond valuation, capital budgeting, earnings per share of ownership, and capital structure and financial leverage. As these perhaps arcane terms may suggest, there is a vast array of tools for financial analysis that are foreign to the mental health professional, but they can be helpful in business planning.

Mental health practitioners often do not appreciate the significance of wisely managing their taxes. Bradford and Davis (1984) place special emphasis on selecting a tax adviser, noting that a tax adviser goes beyond merely preparing tax returns and helps the practitioner implement tax-saving strategies by explaining and suggesting ways to achieve practice-related goals in advantageous ways. Mental health practitioners should not believe that getting their taxes paid on time is anything but the timely fulfillment of an obligation. The information in the tax return must be accurate and honest, of course, and it must also reflect what the ever changing tax laws require and allow, as well as the mental health practitioner's unique considerations. This means having a tax adviser who is well qualified, probably an up-to-date certified public accountant (CPA), although there are many fine accountants who have not attained CPA status. An attorney who is a tax adviser might have a master's degree in tax law. In any event, a tax adviser should communicate well and have some familiarity with mental health practice. Since this combination of knowledge may be difficult to locate, the best solution is to seek teamwork between the accountants and attorneys who serve the practice in several different specialized ways.

This step of business planning may be expensive, but the cost should not deter action. The Internal Revenue Service deems these expenditures reasonable and necessary for generating business income, and so they are deductible. The mental health practitioner should also view fees for accounting and legal expertise as reasonable and necessary expenditures and gain the entrepreneurial and tax benefits that these services can offer. Given the business and risk-management benefits, expenditures of this kind should be viewed as essential investments.

Finally, step 11 should give the mental health CEO an awareness of how much cash is needed when and for what purpose. This awareness can lead to a search for sources of short- and long-term financing. Whenever finances are involved, a logical rationale should be stated and consideration should be given to alternatives (such as leasing instead of buying equipment).

Step 12: The Contingency Plan. While crises can seldom if ever be predicted with any certainty, there should be a general plan for dealing with them. In Chapter Three, suggestions will be made for managing a crisis. For now, suffice it to say that a crisis-management strategy should be determined proactively. Planning for crises can prime the CEO to deal with them in the practice.

Step 13: The Concluding Summary. Step 13 draws all the critical issues together. Major risks are identified, along with means for managing them. As required by entrepreneurship, the concluding summary posits the benefits to investors. Remember, a mental health business must have a reasonable chance of yielding benefits in many forms, not the least of which is profit.

Using a Business Plan

The mental health CEO uses the business plan as an introduction. It is not an indelibly imprinted game plan; it is not irreversible. On the contrary, it is intended to initiate but not control. It will and should be changed. As it is implemented, it will be supplemented with data from market analyses, independently conducted studies of targeted problems, changes in and adaptations to personnel, and new information about competitors and service specifications.

It is known that most—say, 60 percent to 70 percent—of the money generated by health-care services is allocated to expenditures other than income for the practitioner (Parker, 1987). Obviously, the practitioner's income can be maximized through planned economic moves and expenditures. To attempt to operate without a carefully derived and authoritative business plan is contrary to entrepreneurship and pragmatic logic. The business plan is "simply a formal statement about the direction a practice will take over a fixed period of time with a built-in mechanism to measure success" and it is intended to "enable management to take advantage of new opportunities and changing circumstances" (Forman and Forman, 1987, p. 37). The business plan is a process, never a finalized product. It must remain flexible and be evaluated repeatedly. It helps minimize and avoid problems and maximize and create opportunities. For success, the commitment to business planning must be present in all areas of mental health practice.

CHAPTER 3

Service-Oriented Marketing

REGARDLESS OF THE PROFESSIONAL CHARACTERIS-
tics of the practitioners in the group practice, the success of the
mental health business depends on marketing. Many mental
health practitioners believe—erroneously—that advancing their
skills (such as by new certifications) or having years of experience are tantamount to establishing a successful practice. In
fact, however, there is a threshold of essential skill required for
establishing and maintaining a mental health practice.

The foremost key to success is not skill itself; it is an
astute marketing strategy. This chapter is devoted to clarifying
the nature and fundamental dimensions of marketing. Chapter
Four will deal with specific strategies for promoting the mental
health practice, including advertising in a manner that is consonant both with professionalism and with the aggressive pursuit
of success.

Most basically, entrepreneurship, as defined here, places
marketing at the heart of the organization. Marketing initiates
the system that generates the lifeblood of the practice—namely,
income. Of course, income depends on varied processes and
components determined by the profession and the marketplace.
Pledged to entrepreneurship, the mental health CEO must be
ever vigilant that the chosen marketing approach furthers efficacious business operations, promotes short- and long-term
organizational benefits, and honors the role of professionalism
in the health care industry.

Toward a Definition of Marketing

Marketing is more than advertising. It is a system that pervades the entire enterprise, including its organizational and operational aspects. Marketing promotes the establishment, maintenance, development, and protection of the mental health practice.

Marketing may be defined as a system—that is, it is more than the sum of its parts. Marketing also casts a framework around the business environment and its operations. As Mahon (1978, p. 117) describes it:

> Marketing is an aura that pervades an organization and everyone in it. It is a will to expand and grow and *to be of service.* Indeed, marketing ranks with finance and production as one of the topmost functions of a business, and in some respects it is the most important of all. For it provides the organizational spark that ignites the principal systems and functions, and it monitors their progress. It originates the business plan as to what shall be produced, where and how it will be sold, and within limits, at what price. It is the principal interface between an organization and its markets. More than any other function, it seeks to expand volume and profits by ascertaining the needs and demands of customers and clients, and satisfying them [emphasis in original].

While Mahon calls marketing an "aura," many marketing specialists point to a state of mind or a professional service orientation. For example, Felton (1959, p. 55) describes marketing as "a corporate state of mind that insists on the integration and coordination of all of the marketing functions which, in turn, are melded with other corporate functions, for the basic objective of producing maximum long-range corporate profits." Konopa and Calabro (1971) emphasize that marketing seeks to produce an external consumer orientation and an integration of organizational and operational efforts.

Definitions of marketing recognize that the processes zero in on clients' satisfaction. Given mental health professionals' traditional altruism, satisfying clients is very appealing, and marketing concepts are directed toward this goal (McCarthy and Perreault, 1984). Winter (1985, pp. 69–70) states, "Marketing is a process that aims to create a perception or image of an organization and its services or products to a targeted consumer market. It is a process that aims to facilitate an exchange of resources [that] through new and regenerating business will lead to increases in an organization's market share." Clearly, generating business is a primary dimension of marketing, but there are other dimensions as well.

Accommodation of clients is front and center in decision making about what targeted markets want and need (Kotler, 1980). "The marketing concept . . . calls for most of the effort to be spent on discovering the wants of a target audience and then creating the goods and services to satisfy them" (Kotler and Zaltman, 1971, p. 5). While satisfying the client may be a shibboleth of the mental health marketing community, there are other considerations. These include profit, self-fulfillment (including altruism) for the practitioners, and perpetuation of the organization for an array of benefits. On the basis of a thoughtful and scholarly analysis of the marketing concept, Houston (1986, p. 85) concludes, "The marketing concept is a managerial prescription relating to the attainment of an entity's goals. For certain well-defined but restrictive market conditions and for exchange-determined goals which are not product related, the marketing concept is a prescription showing how an entity can achieve these goals most efficiently. . . . The marketing concept states that an entity achieves its own exchange-determined goals most efficiently through a thorough understanding of potential exchange partners and their needs and wants, through a thorough understanding of the costs associated with satisfying those needs and wants, and then designing, producing, and offering products in light of this understanding."

It is of special relevance to mental health practitioners that what clients express as needs and wants should not automatically be accepted as dictates. In keeping with the preventive objective of mental health services, it is possible and appropriate to educate consumers—that is, to shape the needs and wants that will later become the subjects of marketing strategies. The long-term view for marketing a mental health practice should include consideration of what will be helpful both to the consumer and to the mental health organization. In other words, the mental health marketer can create a need that will further the interests of his or her practice (a need that would, of course, be subject to approval from public policy as a constructive and healthful addition to or change for the marketplace).

Adapting a Product View to a Professional Service

Service providers of any ilk, including mental health practitioners, commonly display a knee-jerk reaction to language and ideas about marketing that were birthed in product marketing. They believe that marketing a professional service is surely different from marketing a product. Marketing a professional service is different from marketing a product, but there are far more commonalities than differences.

The "tangible versus intangible" distinction is of legitimate concern. Products are tangible. They occupy space, can be seen and touched, and have properties that lend themselves to objective assessment. Professional services, by contrast, are intangible. They rely on senses and perception, have idiosyncratic constructs, can be valued only by the receiver, and defy objective appraisal. It is a matter of a physical state (tangible) versus a mental state (intangible).

Too often, the outcome is a belief that professional services cannot be marketed: "Intangibility has been widely accepted as a barrier to marketing in the service sector. Proven strategies of product marketing cannot be applied when the 'product' being marketed cannot be seen, felt, or guaranteed to provide specific measurable results" (Van Doren and Relle,

1987, p. 31). That product marketing is not adaptable to service marketing is a false assumption. It is necessary, of course, to make conceptual and strategic accommodations. Van Doren and Relle suggest transforming intangible services into tangible objects, such as through the use of brochures, reports, written documents, and so on. This action is intended to help the service provider accept that a tangible-intangible blend is possible.

Intangibility is but one of numerous distinctions between product and service marketing; Webster (1987) points out several others.

1. Services are the most intimately linked to delivery of satisfaction.
2. More than assembling parts for delivery, services represent a mix of physical facilities and mental and physical labor.
3. Consumption of services is most dependent on the consumer's judgment.
4. Services are evaluated during consumption, while products are evaluated afterward.
5. Services cannot be inventoried, and service marketers must match demand levels to capacity.
6. Services typically lack physical distribution channels; instead, they emphasize scheduling or service delivery (more than locations or facilities).
7. Service businesses face their greatest challenge in determining their fixed and operating costs.
8. It is more difficult for a service to obtain data on competitive performance.

The distinctions are outweighed by the similarities. Just as a psychodynamic therapist can benefit from understanding the behavior therapist's ideas (and vice versa), so can the service marketer benefit from the ideas of the product marketer. The transformation of product-based ideas into service-based ideas is the key to entrepreneurship, which has its basis in pragmatism. Throughout this book (but particularly in this chapter and in Chapter Four), the information for marketing professional services is a transposition of valid and reliable ideas and strategies used in other marketing realms; neither intangibility nor professionalism negates their usefulness.

On Competition

Mental health professionals have long espoused the value of professional collegiality. While practitioners believe in upgrading their qualifications to gain coveted professional stature, they may be reluctant to abandon academic collegiality in favor of embracing the business value of competition. Today, it is possible and preferable for mental health professionals to blend the two vantage points.

As mentioned earlier, successful mental health practice does not depend only on advanced professional training, esteemed credentials, or years of experience. In the business world, rightly or wrongly, an entry-level set of these factors is necessary for establishment and maintenance of a mental health practice, but it is not sufficient for a successful practice. As much as anything, marketing is the answer.

Marketing gives consideration to what others are doing in the same marketplace. In other words, a marketing approach analyzes how other mental health professionals operate in the same community and elsewhere. While these other practitioners, both near and far, are competitors, they need not be viewed as the enemy.

For conceptualizing competition among mental health practitioners, consider the following: "The notion that superior performance requires a business to gain and hold an advantage over competitors is central to contemporary strategic thinking. Businesses seeking advantage are exhorted to develop distinctive competencies and manage for lowest delivered costs or differentiation through superior customer value. The promised payoff is market share dominance and profitability above average for the industry" (Day and Wensley, 1988, p. 1). Much of this stance is justified; it is possible to use competitors in a constructive, nonhostile manner. In fact, for risk-management purposes, it is far better to stay in the good graces of competitors by promoting an exchange of information (but not giving away trade secrets) than to avoid contact with them. A competitor in the community with whom there has been little or no positive contact is the most apt to step forward to encourage or assist a disgruntled former client in an ethical, regulatory, or legal complaint.

Constructive Competition. Competition can be constructive. This position assumes that competition is not to be eliminated— it can be a source of incomparable benefit. In fact, it may be self-destructive (for multiple reasons) to try to destroy the competition: "Taking business away from your competitors is one way to achieve growth. However, this situation may create problems for the entire industry. Your competitors will usually react quickly if they lose business to your company, and this creates an unstable situation in which problems are likely to occur. A better way to achieve growth is to expand your market. Rather than fighting competitors for the same pool of customers, concentrate on finding new customers. If you are competing in a market of many small businesses . . . , you can grow by introducing something new which makes your business different from the rest" (Meredith, Nelson, and Neck, 1982, p. 171). This view is especially appropriate in the mental health professions and will be the underlying premise throughout the marketing strategies offered here. (As we soon shall see, it is possible for mental health service competitors to offer one another support through an alliance.)

Comparative Analysis of Competitors. It seems self-evident that one can learn much by knowing how one's competitors operate. From a survey of marketing directors in hospitals, Winston (1986b, p. 7) reports that "over 97% indicated negative to (1) possessing any formal model for evaluating competition; (2) being able to use a decision-support system for modeling or strategy development; and (3) over 92% indicated most strategies were done by 'gut-feelings' rather than by any competitor analysis. It has become apparent that competitor analysis systems will need to be developed in the future and become integrated into our marketing planning processes."

As befits their training in behavioral science methodologies, mental health professionals should be prepared upon entry into the field to garner data in a manner that will provide useful information about and insight into the operations of their competitors. The premise is that competitive mental health professionals in the community will provide an important comparative source for marketing. Using information from or about them (obtained by whatever ethical and legal means), the mental health CEO can make comparative analyses of costs, needs of prospective clients, marketing indices, and promotional prognoses. For example, readily obtainable information about comparable clinical practices—number and qualifications of staff members, referral sources, promotional techniques, and types of clients—can be invaluable for business and marketing planning. It is usually helpful to understand the competitor's resources, whether these take the form of qualifications and skills or financial backing. The goal is to learn from the competition and to build the proverbial better mousetrap.

Comparative Analysis Through Clients. Another form of analysis of the competition can come from the practice's own clients. A client-focused assessment of what they received versus what they would have received from a competitor can reveal strengths, weaknesses, and marketing alternatives. This analysis starts with an end-use segment—that is, a sample of clients who have completed or left treatment—with consideration given to whether an intervention has been a success or a failure. The analysis then works backwards, through the connecting links, to the intake stage and identifies what caused certain effects at critical points, what could or should have occurred for a better service and marketing result, and what will be needed in the future to improve service. Then a comparison (admittedly conjectural) gauges how a competitor would have performed with the same sort of client. As a final step, consideration is given to what impact the preferred systemic changes would have on resources, both outgoing and incoming.

Forming an Alliance with Competitors. Competition does not necessarily mean the dismantling of academic values or the destruction of relationships with colleagues. On the contrary, professional alliances can be formed among competitors.

The fundamental idea is that unnecessary competition should be replaced by cooperation that will further everyone's marketing goals. An alliance, by definition, is a confederation. Between organizations, it is often created by formal agreement. In a mental health services community, it may or may not be wise or necessary to have an agreement; many benefits can accrue to all members through a simple, good-faith understanding. Further, a good-faith understanding is always subject to change, probably more than a formal agreement is, and can thus be modified without undue effort when market conditions call for a change. An alliance need not be forever; it exists only to serve a marketing purpose, and this charter is understood by all the allies.

The 1980s health-care industry has witnessed a surge of collectives, many of which are in the vein of professional alliances. While there are various structures and versions, the most prominent form is the health maintenance organization (HMO). Whether a mental health professional or practice group wishes, needs to, or should be affiliated with an HMO is an individual decision that depends on evaluation of the benefits and detriments. Cunningham and Bennett (1987) describe HMOs' development and their current competitive status. They offer marketing information about the strengths and weaknesses of HMO-based health care (such as would assist the mental health CEO's determination of whether his or her practice should accept or reject an alliance with an HMO).

Since a mental health alliance is restricted to certain objectives and is subject to modification, it should be thought of as a limited alliance. The mental health CEO should not allow dilution of the entrepreneurial goals for his or her practice. The alliance is for a limited purpose and time.

In a mental health alliance, two or more practice groups recognize that each can be more successful with cooperation from the other(s). Consequently, group A will choose to give emphasis to service 1 and x-type clients, while group B will choose to allow that turf to group A and will instead give emphasis to service 2 and y-type clients. Group A in turn will show deference to group B for the latter's service and type of client. The real benefit comes not only from avoiding competition for the same market sector but also from creating complementarity.

Professional complementarity can take several forms. One is simply not to speak ill of the competition. While usually informal, the supportive arrangement can be formal and may be reflected in shared advertisements in a telephone directory listing practitioners with the same service interests (for example, this is often done by members of the American Association for Marriage and Family Therapy). Another form involves referrals. It is good business to refer clients sometimes, even when the clients could have been served by the referring party. Probably the best form of professional complementarity is achieved when, say, two groups decide that each will definitely (or usually) channel a particular type of client or service need to the other one. A professional alliance does more than manage the competition. It is an effective means of using resources. It can also make marketing and promotion more cost-effective.

Marketing and the Service-Delivery System

Marketing cannot be separated from clinical services. "Marketing personnel often play a coordinating role, linking demands from outside the organization with the functional departments inside the firm that are capable of satisfying those demands" (Ruekert and Walker, 1987, p. 1). The mental health CEO cannot be divorced from marketing (see Chapter Nine), and the dynamics of the mental health practice group (see Chapter Six) are best nurtured by inputs from members in as many aspects of the organization as possible.

Marketing has two directions: outward, to the public marketplace, and inward, to the group members, whether they are professionals or support staffers. Individual goals are commonly discrepant with organizational goals, and the marketing plan must deal with this conflict-prone situation to avoid cleavage or dissonance. A reasonable systemic message is the following (Ruekert and Walker, 1987, p. 2): "Because people in each functional area have distinct skills, resources, and capabilities, they are functionally interdependent. For marketing and other personnel to do their jobs, there must be exchanges of money, materials, information, technical expertise, and other resources. Each member of the system is dependent on the performance of others, both for the accomplishment of tasks that serve as inputs or preconditions for their own specialized functions and for the ultimate attainment of common goals." The point is that clinical services cannot survive without marketing. Marketing in turn cannot be fruitful without support from the functional (professional and support) personnel.

What is needed is an integrated internal marketing program that will lead members to understand, accept, and enhance the organization's service mix. For example, the mental health CEO should lead each professional and support staff member to take pride in the practice group's unique talents and abilities, be aware of opportunities for service and business expansion, and develop marketing and practice skills themselves.

According to Wheatley (1987), marketing and functional operations can be integrated in the following ways.

1. Have everyone contribute ideas for (say) a positioning statement or a marketing plan.
2. Allocate authority to specific "inside" persons to get the marketing job done (Wheatley speaks negatively of committee attempts and informality).
3. Identify specializations that will motivate the professionals to sell.
4. Assign members specific developmental functions and reward them for concrete attainments (mental health practices are prone to reward members inadequately for nonclinical activities).
5. Maintain a continuing professional development program that will further technical and internal marketing.

6. Budget for time and experiences in a way that is aligned with business and marketing, not just with professional (clinical) skill building.
7. Make a member's career development (rewards, opportunities, and retention) contingent on his or her contributions to the marketing program (which will mean reporting, recording, and evaluating his or her efforts).
8. Keep members informed about what "top management" is considering, planning, and doing.
9. Enrich member's continuing development, perhaps by requiring attendance at seminars, even though it is an expense to the organization.

In keeping with the word *system*, the marketing of a mental health service is developmental and conceptually interconnected: "Beginning with quality research and planning which will focus and direct the institution, it can then move on to the process of 'Internal Marketing' and aligning, educating, and motivating staff towards institutional objectives. The next stage is product development and promotion and finally . . . sale[s] or service delivery where internal marketing and development will serve to aid in the successful close of [a] sales (exchange) transaction" (Winter, 1985, pp. 70–71).

MacStravic (1986, p. 47) suggests using marketing circles, which involve professional and support staff members in the development of structure, allocations, information, motivation, and a host of other necessary conditions: "Small groups of people meet together voluntarily but regularly to examine feedback on past performance and discuss ways to improve outcomes." While the mental health CEO is vested with the entrepreneurial leadership, successful marketing must be directed to professional and support staff members. It is their acceptance and endorsement that will propel the practice toward attainment of its objectives and goals.

Market Positioning

Another fundamental preparation for a market analysis involves market positioning: "When a firm or provider establishes and maintains a distinctive place for itself and its offerings in the market, it is said to be successfully positioned. In the increasingly competitive services sector, effective positioning is one of marketing's most critical tasks" (Shostack, 1987, p. 34). As is readily evident, market positioning is compatible with the view of competition discussed earlier. Effective marketing of mental health services is predicated on establishing the best possible market position, as opposed to a frontal attack on the competition.

In considering a market position, the mental health marketer (presumably the CEO) will look to the complexity of the service-delivery system. This necessitates analysis of the number of points and their intricate connectors in the service-performance sequence. Market positioning must reflect the true nature of the service-delivery system, as will be achieved through definition of the service, business planning, and a comparative analysis of the competition. For example, personal-professional interests could lead a mental health CEO to offer services to children, but a market analysis could reveal that this sector is already well served. To enter the children's sector successfully, it would be necessary for the CEO to ascertain how his or her services could complement existing services in that market. Even then, it may be necessary to delimit services to a particular subgroup or area (for example, court-related cases involving children). Of course, once a market position has been gained and solidified, it can serve as a competitive springboard into other market positions that otherwise would have been foreclosed.

Consideration is also given to the divergence of services. *Low divergence* refers to standardized operations; *high divergence* refers to unique operations. Unique, or high-divergence, operations may be appealing for their stimulating effect, but they are more expensive to create and maintain. For example, offering services to children, adolescents, and adults alike may be appealing, but the high divergence would require extra resources and effort, as compared to a more focused scope of service. Standard, or low-divergence, operations are routine and probably require the least output of new or progressive resources. For example, being a general practitioner of marriage and family therapy has a broad market appeal and requires predictable resources, but the lack of distinction from the competition may be a problem. Standard operations make up the bulk of services for the competition; thus, consumers' perceptions of these operations foster minimal attraction to the particular mental health practice. For effective market positioning, what is needed is a level of divergence that both maximizes consumers' tendency to use the practice and minimizes resource allocations.

Probably the most important aspect of establishing a market positioning is to recognize that it is never truly achieved. Positioning is a permanent objective of marketing and will reflect service development throughout the life of the mental health practice. When the practitioner has an idea for a select type of clinical service or clientele, planning moves to the *development* stage for design of the service-delivery system and the relevant market positioning. As the practice is clarified and promotional strategies are formulated and implemented, there is an *evaluation* stage. The market is tested, and the findings justify adjustments in market positioning. Refinement, or *fine tuning*, continues as services are readied for the full-blown operations of the *introduction* stage. The practice has ongoing status, with continual evaluations for logical repositioning. As payoffs diminish, the *sunsetting* stage requires market positioning for the dissolution of the mental health practice. If the mental health CEO intends to enter a new form of the practice or another venture, the market positioning can aid the transition.

Understanding the Current Marketing Situation

A third fundamental in preparing for a marketing analysis is to formulate a summary of the current or existing marketing situation. It primes the mental health CEO for the marketing tasks ahead. Understanding of the current market is designed to occur along with description of services and business planning, which can be used to generate a comparative analysis of the competition with the present composition of the practice. The next step is to conduct a full-fledged market analysis.

Analysis of the current marketing situation involves five

appraisals (Parker, 1987). First, *the market should be described.* This first appraisal explores five areas: the estimated probable size of the potential client base; the characteristics or makeup of the types of clients who will be targeted by or apt to be attracted to the practice; sources of referrals, including people who are known to refer to other practices; logistics, such as the time required for processing and waiting for services; and clients' impressions, such as about convenience and the staff's care (questionnaires will be helpful). Second, *the service should be specified:* What are the specialties and skills represented by the professionals, what support staffers are available, what is the outlook for profitability, and what new services will be implemented? Third, *consideration is given to information about the competition,* such as who the major competitors are, competitors' strengths and weaknesses, and what the competition means to the CEO's practice. Fourth, *the distribution or service-delivery system must be understood,* perhaps by means of a flowchart or diagram. Fifth, *the macroenvironment is appraised:* What are the current marketplace trends, what is the local population growth or decline, and what are the changing demographics? With this written summary in mind, the mental health CEO is prepared to move to the all-important market analysis.

Conducting a Market Analysis

Marketing is a system, an interweaving of factors that are interdependent and reciprocally influential. Moreover, marketing is never completed: It must exist and be modified throughout the life of the professional service organization. The assessment of marketing strategies and their effects will always be present and will constitute a major responsibility for the mental health CEO. Finally, successful marketing will require contributions from all professional and support staff members of the practice group.

Strategic Marketing. Strategic marketing has four basic stages (Barnes, 1986). First, there is the recognition of a need (which may be implanted and/or cultivated in the consumer's mind).

As mentioned earlier, the mental health service provider typically prefers to be responsive to clients' expressed needs, but public policy also allows a professional to promote engendered needs, as long as that effort promotes human welfare and stays within ethical and legal bounds. Second, a limited personal search is made of service information possessed and transmitted by consumers. Third, operations are standardized, with consideration given to mainline variables (clients' expectations) and peripheral variables (facilities). Fourth, evaluation allows for policy and strategy changes (often change is derived from clients' satisfaction, as objectified by revenues).

The four strategic marketing stages allow the construction of a profile of the professional service providers. The characteristics of each mental health service provider are tempered by environmental features (client-to-professional ratio, competition), which produce an impact on the provider (hours worked, overhead, investment benefits) and on the client (quality and personalization of service, convenience, costs) (Hill and Fannin, 1986). In other words, the marketing analysis starts with data about the functional framework surrounding the delivery of services.

A marketing strategy must be based first of all on reality; idealism is always secondary and controlled. Some mental health professionals, in their quest for success, fly into unjustified optimism or fall into distortions of true conditions in the marketplace. This zeal is often a means of coping with the anxiety produced by uncertainty.

Rather than unabashed optimism devoid of reality, the better and more pragmatic response to anxiety about entrepreneurial or business success is a wise selection of marketing strategies. A marketing strategy must manage forces coming from the interplay among the client, the competition, and the practice: "A good marketing strategy should be characterized by: (a) clear market definition; (b) a good match of corporate strengths and the needs of the market; and (c) superior performance, relative to the competition, in the key success factors of the business" (Webster, 1987, p. 20).

Marketing strategies can be placed into five categories

(Mahon, 1978). First, the *services offered* are periodically re-examined, new services are determined, the size of the client base for new services is estimated, the share of the market earned by present services is determined, written goals and policies are established, and specific client groups to be served are defined. Second, *communication* is based on the development of an overall informational approach, identifying major sources of service users and selecting methods to reach them by marketing. In support of communication, specific informational approaches should be developed, such as brochures, health-information materials, public relations lectures and seminars, television and radio appearances, and so on (more will be said on these kinds of promotional strategies in Chapter Four). Third, *location* efforts analyze the desirability of potential locations and evaluate the volume and trends existing with respect to location, the goal being to determine the need for change (more will be said on strategies in this category in Chapter Seven). Fourth, *fee structure* evaluates policies in a systematic way, including accounts management (Chapter Seven) and risk management (Chapter Eight). Fifth, *market research* evaluates clients' needs (whether expressed or engendered), studies why clients choose and purchase services, determines who influences the selection of services, trains and motivates practice members to communicate effectively with clients, determines the image held of the practice and its staff members by clients and others (general public, referral sources, competitive practitioners), and studies profit trends according to service and client categories.

The Marketing Mix. To select strategies within these five categories, it is necessary to define a *marketing mix.* As Webster (1987, pp. 19–20) describes it:

> One element of the marketing mix is the *product*, which is the professional service. Every product should have its own marketing strategy. The development of such a strategy involves identifying a target market segment, and then developing a marketing program to deliver that product to members

of the segment . . . . A second element of the marketing mix is *price*, the professional's fee. The pricing policy is important because profitability is more related to the respective net margin of a large number of services than to total revenues. The third element is *promotion*, the ways of communication. Each professional service firm should actively seek its own promotional mix, combining those activities that the firm finds suitable. Finally, the remaining element is *place*, where the services can be offered [emphasis in original].

The marketing mix encompasses strategies that can move an idea for clinical service through development, evaluation, test marketing, introduction, ongoing provision, calculated alterations, and dissolution. In other words, the marketing mix has multiple forces, progresses through stages of organizational development, is subject to change, and reflects decisions about allocating resources. The latter will include a *tentative budget mix* necessary to fund the various promotional strategies that have been selected. The marketing mix and the budget mix are predicated on a market audit, a careful analysis of factors that influence success and that can be relied on in making decisions about practical promotional strategies.

The Market Audit. The market analysis is ongoing and will be tailored to the circumstances unique to the practice. Consequently, there is no one set of procedures to which the mental health CEO can turn. Forman and Forman (1987), however, offer a valuable approach to assessing consumers, competition, and capability. Rather than the term *market analysis*, they prefer the term *market audit* and suggest data collection according to the format shown in Exhibit 1. While objective and quantifiable data are preferable, they are not essential. What is essential is the willingness of the mental health CEO (and preferably all others in the practice, professional and support staffers alike) to garner data continually for a market analysis or audit. The lack of easy-to-use assessment methods must not deter a thought-

Exhibit 1. Market Audit.

I.   The Market
     A.   Geographical Location
          1.   What is it?
          2.   How big is it?
          3.   How is it divided?
     B.   Segmentation
          1.   What are the bases for segmenting?
          2.   On what basis were they divided?
               a.   Ease of identification
               b.   Potential for serving
               c.   Adequate demand
               d.   Economic accessibility
               e.   Reactivity to marketing efforts
          3.   What are the demographic and psychographic charac-
               teristics?
          4.   From which sources was information obtained?
               a.   Own research
               b.   University
               c.   Mental health authority
               d.   Health planning board
               e.   Utility company
               f.   Government office
               g.   Chamber of commerce
               h.   *Sales and Marketing Management*
               i.   Other
          5.   What factors limit your potential market?
     C.   Demand
          1.   What demand exists?
          2.   What strategies are required?
II. The Competition
     A.   How many competitors are there now?
     B.   In what segments are they competing?
     C.   What specific services are offered by your competitors?
     D.   What advantages do you have over your competitors?
     E.   What advantages do your competitors have over you?
     F.   What new sources of competition do you anticipate?
III. Opportunities and Threats
     A.   Environmental Elements
          1.   Technological innovations
          2.   Governmental regulations
          3.   Economy
          4.   Culture
          5.   Population demographics
          6.   Levels of each demand state
          7.   Your image

(continued on next page)

Exhibit 1. Market Audit, Cont'd.

     B. Organizational Elements in Your Practice
         1.   Structure
         2.   Systems
         3.   Tasks
         4.   Personnel
         5.   Culture
IV. Marketing Strategy
     A. Description of Your Marketing Strategy
     B. Alternative Strategy for Your Practice Objectives

Source: Adapted from Forman and Forman, 1987, pp. 53–54.

ful, data-based analysis. Certainly entrepreneurship in general, and better business techniques in particular, require an astute market analysis.

Targeting a Market Segment. Regardless of structure or formality, a market analysis should use segment descriptors. The marketing strategies selected are influenced considerably by the needs and makeup of the targeted market segment(s). According to Ray (1982, p. 116), "People can be described and put into segments in many ways. This can be done on the basis of (1) where they live, (2) their socio-economic class, (3) their personality, (4) their product-oriented [or service-oriented] problems and needs, (5) their product [or service] usage rates and characteristics, and (6) their brand [or practice group] loyalty. All of these types of segmenting *descriptors* are useful in particular situations and for particular communication element decisions." According to Bell (1972), a segment should be analyzed for ease of identification, potential as a market, sufficiency of demand, economic accessibility, and distinctive reactivity to marketing efforts.

It is logical to base a segment analysis on factors unique to the community, service, and practice group. Forman and Forman (1987, p. 56) write, "There is an almost unlimited number of ways to segment a market into meaningful clusters. These include segmenting by geography, diagnostic categories, common problems, age, gender, income groups, hobbies, patterns of consumption, price sensitivities, benefits sought, and combination of categories. In order to determine what the market population's characteristics are in ways that can be useful for developing a market strategy, it's helpful to classify them as either demographic or psychographic." Whatever the form of data relied on, data should be as objective as possible, for the results will depend on the quality of the data.

The goal of determining a market segment is to reach as many of the right people as possible for the lowest expenditure of resources. If a marketing message reaches the right people, appropriate self-selection will be implanted in the consumers—that is, it is likely that contact will be made primarily by clients who need the practitioner's unique services and can meet the requirements of the practice (for example, ability to pay). This will benefit the practitioner in many ways, not the least of which will be a prefacing and shaping set for clients' satisfaction.

Defining and choosing target segments is of great importance for mental health services. Most mental health practitioners see themselves as generalists. They may want to treat anyone who walks in the door, but this attitude may be unwise for marketing and risk-management reasons. The choice of a market segment should be based on objective data, a narrowing of focus, and a maximizing of resources. This "specialist" thrust allows studied progress and optimal chances of organizational success.

Many sources of data are useful in a market analysis. For example, Baty (1981) recommends considering the following:

- Library research
- Questionnaire surveys (using a structured questionnaire or interview)
- Existing research reports (investment advisory services)
- Published market statistics
- Trade or professional association meetings (which often yield information about competitors' activities)
- Experts (consultants, university researchers, and specialists, particularly in financial matters)
- Phantom services (with due consideration of ethics, obtain-

ing market data by announcing a nonexistent or prototype service—for example, issuing a press release about a complimentary information booklet on a particular mental health service)

- Professional surveys (using a market research firm).

Another form of market analysis can come from analyzing referrals that have produced clients for the practice group. In their study of physicians' marketing, Parsons and Tomkinson (1987, p. 26) assert that five factors influence a physician to refer a patient: "(1) degree to which past patient references were met by the consulting physician, (2) number of reciprocations the physician receives, (3) communication the physician receives about the referral, (4) previous use of and satisfaction with consulting physician by the patient and the patient's family, and (5) physician's personal knowledge about the consultant and the consultant's personality." Numerous promotional strategies spring readily to mind, not the least of which is giving each referral source feedback about the service provided to the client. There are also implications for market analysis, namely a consideration of how well the mental health practice can satisfy potential referral sources relevant to these five criteria. In other words, fulfillment of the criteria with a referral segment (for example, a medical specialty) will generate a strong market, whereas inability to fulfill them (for example, not being able to reciprocate with referrals) will probably lead to a weak market.

Psychographics. When considering possible market segments, many mental health professionals probably pick up a telephone directory and look at the yellow pages to see what other mental health practitioners are providing in the community and then rely on a seat-of-the-pants estimate of how well the needs of the market are being fulfilled. A next step might be to collect demographic or other data (such as from health-care organizations) that could shed some light on financial conditions (average income, prevalence of health insurance) in the catchment area or on particular client characteristics (a therapist for children should certainly be interested in the birth rate). Usually this analysis is nominal, and the selection of a market segment is based more on personal preference than on data.

Marketing does have one approach with special appeal to mental health professionals: *psychographics.* All types of descriptors are combined to derive insights into the type of person who should typify the targeted market segment. Winston (1983/84) suggests locating data for psychological attributes, life-style variables, purchasing variables, and perceptions of goods and services. These data lead to insight, which is the foundation for the selection of promotional strategies and resource allocations for communications (for example, advertising). Psychographic segmentation relies on personality and benefit descriptors, as might be assessed by questionnaires on attitudes, interests, and opinions. It also uses virtually any other type of relevant and material information that may be useful for giving a life-style portrayal of the potential clientele.

By means of applied social psychology, a psychographic analysis is used to produce a profile of relevant market segments. According to Forman and Forman (1987), this is the strategy of choice for determining the propensity of *demand* (for clinical services), revealing *negative demands* (dislikes for clinical services), supporting *conversional marketing* strategies (to improve market segment opinions, overcome biases, and correct misinformation), uncover *latent demands* (sensed or perceived, but unexpressed, needs), accommodate *developmental marketing* (progressive strategies to detect and meet unmet needs), recognize *irregular demands* (fluctuating need states that may lead to faulty marketing decisions), and facilitate *synchromarketing* (coordination and integration of supply and demand).

Within psychographic segmentation there is *attitude-structure analysis.* This form of analysis combines benefits, usage, and loyalty descriptors to allow the mental health CEO to estimate how potential clients might be benefited, how they would probably perceive services, and which ones they would prefer. Attitude-structure analysis can be used to establish behavioral modification strategies, such as for enhancing public perceptions of the mental health professions, the members of the practice, and different types of services (including those to be offered by the practice).

An attitude-structure analysis relies on the mental health CEO's ability to discern critical data, which may be nebulous or ambiguous. Ray (1982, p. 131) offers a four-step plan (see Exhibit 2). If the product-marketing language of Exhibit 2 is translated into service-marketing language, the exhibit constitutes a viable guide to conducting an attitude-structure analysis for a market analysis of mental health services. For example, an attitude-structure analysis would pinpoint groups or types of per-

Exhibit 2. Plan for Attitude-Structure Analysis.

1. Define groups that differ in past or future propensity to consume the product, use the service, or act on the idea you are supporting. This can be done by questionnaire, by past sales . . . , and by general analysis.

2. Determine the perceptions of the different preference-consumption groups formed in the first step. This, again, can be done tentatively and can be based on the judgment and experience of the analyst, or this judgment can be tempered by marketing research data. The kind of perception information necessary has two general parts: (a) perceptions relevant to the product class, the attributes sought, and the relative importance of the attributes in the product or service category; and (b) the perceptions of the individual brands or company offerings that are related to the product-class offerings. Thus, the assumption here is that the product-class perceptions define the buyer's need, and the perceptions of the brands indicate how well each brand fulfills the need.

3. Adjust the preference groups established in the first step by the perception information developed in the second step. The goal is to establish homogeneous groups. The theory here is that buyers will prefer those products and brands they see as fitting their needs, and so the different purchasing groups formed in the first step should be homogeneous in terms of the perception analysis of the second step. But it may be that groups with slightly lower or higher propensity to consume may be brought into the main ones on the basis of their perceptions, or it may be that the main preference groups have embedded in them more than one perception group, and so the groups may have to be split.

4. Analyze the resulting segments in terms of their typical purchase-and-use behavior and resultant communication needs.

Source: Adapted from Ray, 1982, p. 131.

sons (consumers) in the market who potentially need mental health services, and it would determine how these people view service alternatives, assessing an array of attitudes and preferences (for individual versus group treatment, psychodynamic versus behavioral interventions, treatment by a psychologist versus by a social worker, service in a medical versus a nonmedical context, and so on). On this basis, and with consideration of the objectives and resources of the practice, the mental health CEO would fashion a marketing plan and select promotional strategies to synthesize market segments that would be compatible with the services.

Communication in Marketing

Most promotional strategies, such as advertising, depend on effective communication. In fact, communication may well determine the overall success of a mental health practice. For example, if the mental health CEO were to conduct an image survey (a helpful tool for market analysis) of how other professionals and laypersons view his or her practice, "the problems unearthed in a survey of a firm's standing with its publics will often be found to be communications-related" (Mahon, 1978, p. 143).

The nature of therapeutic interactions certainly requires effective communication. Discussing consultation, Brown, Pryzwansky, and Schulte (1987, p. 104) say, "Sensing mechanisms are necessary, but communication of what is seen or heard is key to organizational adaptability," and they posit a relationship between consultation and lateral communication (between equal units) and vertical communication (between components in an organizational hierarchy). Discussing psychological reports, Ownby (1987, p. xii) holds as an initial postulate that their "primary purpose . . . is to communicate to a referral agent or agents information about a client in a way which will result in change in the referral agent's beliefs about or behavior toward the client." Discussing psychotherapy, Tyler (1969, p. 38) asserts, "The main *skill* a counselor must develop is that of communicating his understanding of what the client is trying to express" (emphasis in original). Communication is fundamental to mental health services, yet it is often ignored in mental health marketing.

Within the mental health organization (Chapter Five) and in all promotional strategies (Chapter Four), there must be a commitment to communication. For example, the cultivation of referral sources is often better achieved through personal communications (a thank-you note or a brief feedback report on service provided to a client) than through the "wining and dining" so often (but erroneously) thought necessary for obtaining future business.

One purpose of communication is to reach the public. So-called public relations is commonly thought of as image building. For professional services marketing, public relations strategy is far more than "puffing" sterling qualities; in mental health services, a "puffing" approach usually provides more neurotic (egocentric) need fulfillment for the marketer than marketing benefits for the practice group.

In marketing mental health services, a public relations strategy is intended to educate the marketplace via communications. This approach is certainly compatible with professionalism. In public relations, the communications function is directed toward the broad objectives of retaining current clients, gaining new clients, and expanding the use of services. In a systemic framework, public relations promotes involvement by clients, community and referral sources, and the professional and support staff members of the practice group. To achieve these communication objectives, the mental health CEO guides the practice group toward a strong organizational structure, adequate geographical coverage, a complete service line, high technical competence and quality, specialized expertise, a competitive fee structure, high employee moral, and top ethical standards (Mahon, 1978).

Personalization in Marketing

The intangibility of professional services can raise doubts about the appropriateness of a product-oriented marketing approach, yet countless examples demonstrate how product-oriented principles are adaptable to the marketing of professional services. Nevertheless, the marketing of professional services places special emphasis on *personalization* of services.

A mental health professional spends years becoming a clinician. He or she receives academic training in the nature and usefulness of mental health interventions. Training provides time and guidance for adjusting personal ideas and integrating them with professional ideas about mental health.

It is a different scenario for a person who considers becoming a mental health client. Prospective clients approaching treatment enter unknown territory. They do not know what is expected of them or what to expect from the "shrinks." In fact, mental health services are still viewed by many persons as a court of last resort or a mark of failure, and they attach a stigma to having to be recipients of such services.

With this as a backdrop, the mental health CEO must recognize that clients may be uneasy about receiving and accepting mental health marketing messages. Clients may sense risk or threat when receiving a promotional idea and may not be receptive to information about clinical services: "Consumer behavior involves risk in the sense that any action of a consumer will produce consequences which he cannot anticipate with anything approximating certainty, and some of which at least are likely to be unpleasant" (Bauer, 1960, p. 389). Thus, the marketing mix should include strategies for overcoming consumers' reluctance and increasing their receptivity (Mangold, Berl, Pol, and Abercrombie, 1987). Such strategies may include, for example, arranging for an established client to provide an incoming client with information about the service. Changes in ethical principles (such as for psychologists) may also be ushering in the use of clients' testimonials regarding quality of service (Bales, 1988), which may allay uncertainty on the part of consumers.

After the potential client is sufficiently attracted to the mental health practice to consider receiving services from it, it is crucial to personalize communications. As Surprenant and Solomon (1987, p. 87) write, "In a broad sense, 'personalized service' refers to any behaviors occurring in the interaction intended to contribute to the individuation of the customer. That is, the 'customer' role is embellished in the encounter through specific recognition of the customer's uniqueness as an individual over and above his/her status as an anonymous services recipient." Still promoting marketing goals, the mental health professional (with the support staff in a complementary role) must convey the personality of the organization to the consumer. The practitioner's appearance, demeanor, and skills epitomize and define the services to the prospective client. While the mental health CEO can shape the amount of personalization expected, only the individual practitioner can implement the message.

Surprenant and Solomon (1987, p. 94) conclude that "all forms of personalization do not necessarily result in more positive evaluations of the service offering by consumers," while Nordstrom and Steinke (1987) assert that marketing should recognize that the manner of the professional is the most important determinant of a client's selection of a practitioner, with credentials considered next (convenience, office characteristics, and personal appearance also are considered). To determine what influences the clients who accept services from the practice, Winston (1987, p. 5) recommends using focus groups, where consumers gather to provide a professional with "firsthand feedback about why and how people perceive, utilize, and relate to health services" and an opportunity "to validate and improve other forms of marketing research through demographic, economic, political, social, and value analyses." Winston also provides a pragmatic set of guidelines for focus groups.

Selling in Marketing

Implicit in a client's decision-making process about accepting or rejecting service is that it will be prefaced with sufficient information. Therefore, the mental health professional will have to inform and persuade the client. In practical terms, this amounts to convincing the client of the need for the service, the benefits that can result, and the qualifications of the practitioner to produce the desired results.

The traditional view is that a mental health professional is a helper, with predominantly altruistic motives. This view allows little if any persuasion before a client's personal commitment to treatment (thereafter, of course, persuasion is considered a critical dimension of efficacious therapy). Professionals who adhere to this traditional view are harboring an outdated conceptualization of mental health services, especially services offered in the private sector.

The concept of entrepreneurship embraces the idea that the mental health CEO will lead his or her fellow professionals and support staff members to accept, promote, and provide selling of the services. Indeed, it is impossible to meet sales objectives without professionals' earnest efforts: "In addition to the necessary technical competence and the other basic requisites for professional growth, there usually will be found a 'salesman' or several 'salesmen' who are responsible for bringing in most of the new business. Ideally, the salesman is a knowledgeable member of his profession—a capable practitioner. But, consciously or otherwise, he adapts and applies the same techniques in obtaining visibility for himself and his firm and in selling professional services, as are used by the successful manufacturer or retailer" (Mahon, 1978, p. 5). Cueny, Miller, and Eldridge (1986) recommend that each professional write sales reports (probably monthly descriptions of what has been attempted, what has succeeded and failed, and outcomes) that will be submitted to and reviewed by the other members of the organization. This kind of document will give impetus to the sales dimension and aid in evaluation of personnel, analytical conceptualizing, resource allocation, and business planning.

One technique is to develop a list of all the services that can be provided by the practice. The mental health CEO (or a designee) meets on a periodic basis (perhaps monthly) with each clinical service provider and reviews each current case. During the review, questions are raised about considering the use of other services. For example, a therapist might be so close to the case that he or she fails to recognize how, say, psychological testing could complement the treatment plan. In the process, the therapist gets much-needed supervision, is stimulated to rethink the treatment plan for the benefit of the client, and becomes motivated to persuade the client of the need for additional services. Similar review of past cases may spark a follow-up effort that could lead to benefits for clients and a resumption of services to them.

It is important to point out that the sales dimension constitutes a continuum, running from the invitation (such as an advertisement) to the client's entry into service and throughout his or her service period. Moreover, satisfied clients comprise an important referral and public relations pool, and follow-up efforts should be directed at selling the practice group to clients who have completed treatment. This effort may include, for example, a periodic newsletter to the "alumni" of the practice, telling them about new members of the team, new services, and advances in research. Follow-up will help attract past clients back to the practice in times of need and will motivate them to speak positively of the practice in their contacts with others (potential clients).

Crisis Management in Marketing

Mental health professionals believe in the importance of managing crises in everyday life, at least on an individual basis. Somehow, though, the mental health profession tends to overlook the applicability of crisis management to the private practice.

While risk-management strategies are directed at creating and maintaining conditions that will preclude or minimize the possibility of, say, negative attitudes toward the mental health practice (see Chapter Eight), there is inevitably a risk from the human fallibility of the professional and support staff members. The risk may manifest itself in an errant practitioner's sexual misconduct with a client or in a practitioner's being charged with a crime. Sometimes the problem is unjustified by the standard of care, yet a disgruntled client files a complaint (say, a malpractice suit) that is publicized in a newspaper. The risk may also be manifested in publicity that identifies a client of the practice who has committed suicide or harmed someone else.

Any sort of bad publicity, negative image, or notoriety can affect the marketing program. To avoid or minimize devastating effects, the mental health CEO should develop an approach to crisis management. Winston (1986a, p. 9) offers a practical set of suggestions:

> In order to plan for potential crises, a service organization must (1) keep abreast of [its] services and try to anticipate potential problem areas—i.e., an employee who keeps getting complaints from customers or scattered cases of unsafe products; (2) a plan must be set up to develop a media relations strategy whereby an individual person must respond to the press and a corporate philosophy must be presented and remain constant; (3) information kits can be developed for key employees instructing them how to keep things operating normally even though a crisis occurs; (4) a crisis team could be assigned [as in] disaster planning in hospitals; (5) simulation models could be used to "test" employees on how they would handle situations along the lines of decision-support systems with "what-if" questions and scenarios; (6) key executives who work well under stress and can be patient and calm with the press and public need to be identified and be part of the crisis team; and (7) crises must be taken seriously and not strategized with . . . superficial forms of communication techniques, especially if the crisis is real and the organization is at fault.

Proaction is the byword. It should be recognized that when there is a frontal attack on the reputation of a professional, he or she will understandably experience an escalation of anxiety and thus lose important objectivity. Therefore, while it is necessary to have the mental health professional's input to the crisis management plan, it may be advisable to have the designated spokesperson be someone with less vested interest (such as an attorney or a public relations expert), unless there are means for objective monitoring of the mental health CEO's communications. If managed improperly, a crisis ("bad press") can destroy, in short order, a business or professional reputation that has taken years and vast amounts of money to develop and can curtail profitability for years to come.

An Ethical Framework for Marketing

Given the importance of professional ethics, the marketing of mental health services should be framed to provide a rapprochement between public policy and disciplinary preferences. Contemporary public policy demands that professional ethics go beyond disciplinary preferences and provide for reasonable (if not maximum) consumer preferences and benefits. This mandate has taken form in legal judgments and governmental regulatory efforts to wrest control over advertising, accreditation, certification, and other matters from the exclusive control of professional associations.

This is not to say that the collective voice of a professional discipline will or should go unheeded. Professional associations still serve as useful conduits for practitioners' preferences, but they must be filtered through public policy. At this time, marketing ideas and promotional strategies (such as those presented in this book) are not considered unethical unless they are false and misleading. It is true that some would prefer more restraint on marketing through ethical measures, but this is not to be at present. (Of course, an axiom of both public policy and professionalism is that the future can introduce different expectations and requirements.)

CHAPTER 4

Practical
Promotional Strategies

SYSTEMATIC MARKETING IS ESSENTIAL TO THE ESTAB-
lishment, maintenance, development, and protection of the
mental health practice. To succeed in business, the mental health
CEO must move the practice group to effective competition
with other mental health practitioners who are vying for the
same market sector(s). In other words, effective competition
translates into attracting as many of the *right kind* of clients as
appropriate to the resources and objectives of the mental health
practice. Advantageous market positioning is a prerequisite.
After a market analysis, strategic promotional communications
are directed at the chosen marketing mix. Since there are usually
various types of promotional communications, they form the
promotional mix—that is, a composite of informational and
strategic ideas, methods, and techniques—which is designed to
create in the minds of targeted consumers the reasons why service should be received from the particular mental health practice. Relying on different marketing analysis techniques (market audit, referral analysis, psychographics, attitude-structure
analysis, and so on), the mental health CEO can begin to formulate a promotional system that will transmit personalized
messages and sell the service to prospective clients.

Criticism of Promoting Professional Services

Notwithstanding the surge toward the commercialization
of health-care services, there has been marked reluctance in some

quarters to accept unequivocally the promotion of professional services. Professional associations have tended to brand certain promotional efforts as unethical. With an air of righteous indignation, they have asserted that such marketing efforts as advertising will diminish the dignity of the profession and allow unscrupulous practitioners to succeed over more principled colleagues.

In the 1970's, there was much public and professional criticism of advertising in general: "In recent years, advertising has been under an almost constant barrage of criticism. Advertising has been accused of being misleading, expensive, wasteful, anticompetitive, inflationary, offensive, intrusive, and even immoral" (Bloom, 1976, p. 1). This skepticism led to an increase in laws and regulations governing advertising. Eventually, the American public realized the important benefits of advertising professional services and took its case to the Federal Trade Commission (FTC), which is responsible for monitoring antitrust law.

In *Goldfarb v. Virginia State Bar* (421 U.S. 733, 1975), the U.S. Supreme Court ruled that the professions were not exempt from antitrust laws and were subject to antitrust scrutiny. Over the next few years, the FTC applied much scrutiny to numerous professionals, including attorneys, accountants, real-estate brokers, physicians, dentists, engineers, undertakers, veterinarians, and others. As Overcast, Sales, and Pollard (1982, p. 519) describe it, "In antitrust litigation involving the activities of professional organizations, the courts are primarily concerned with answering the following question: Have the activities of the professional organization significantly impaired the ability of competitive marketing forces to determine (a) the price or fee for professional services, (b) who can enter the market, or (c) the degree of innovation within the profession?" The focus was on, among other things, educational accreditation, professional licensing, specialty certification, restrictions on advertising, and fees and compensation.

In mental health circles, ethical restraints on advertising were highly suspect. In 1977, the Supreme Court ruled that the First Amendment of the U.S. Constitution prohibited professional organizations from unduly restricting their members from advertising their availability and the cost of their services (see *Bates* v. *State Bar of Arizona*, 433 U.S. 350, 1977). In 1979, the FTC held that the American Medical Association's restrictions (such as on advertising that might channel patients to particular physicians and hospitals) were unreasonable and had significant anticompetitive effects (see *American Medical Association* v. *FTC*, 94 F.T.C. 701, final order, October 12, 1979). The FTC (Federal Trade Commission, 1979, p. 917) ruled: "That barrier [the advertising restrictions] has served to deprive consumers of the free flow of information about the availability of health care services, to deter the offering of innovative forms of health care and to stifle the rise of almost every type of health care delivery that could potentially pose a threat to the income of the fee-for-service physicians in private practice. The costs to the public in terms of less expensive or even, perhaps, more improved forms of medical services are great." The FTC attributed less than honorable motives and deleterious social effects to attempts to restrict professional advertising. For physicians' advertising, it came down to this: "In theory, advertising that distributes information can help consumers make better economic decisions" (McDaniel, Smith, and Smith, 1986, p. 134).

Legislatures soon started permitting advertising among licensed professionals (Walker, 1979), and a new public policy emerged: "Competitive markets are considered desirable because they are supposed to provide lower prices, better service, better quality, more frequent innovation, and more efficient use of scarce resources. Competitive markets are also considered desirable because they are supposed to be essentially self-regulating—that is, they are considered less likely to require the development of bureaucratic government regulatory mechanisms to keep them serving the public in a responsible fashion" (Bloom, 1976, p. 2). By the outset of the 1980s, governmental laws and regulations increasingly endorsed promoting the availability and qualities of professional services, including by advertising methods.

Despite the new tenor of legislative efforts and court rulings, certain professional mental health associations, at both the national and state levels, have dogmatically continued to specify what is or is not considered to be ethically proper for advertising and fee-related conditions. For example, the current set of ethics promulgated by the American Psychological Association (1981a, p. 634) recognizes the following idea: "Public statements, announcements of services, advertising, and promotional activities of psychologists serve the purpose of helping the public make informed judgments and choices." Nevertheless, the same document goes on to prescribe and proscribe the information that can be used to describe the provider and the services provided, as well as other conditions that would make a promotional method ethical or potentially unethical. It is known that some state and regional psychological associations still continue to offer guidelines—about what, for example, listings in the yellow pages should contain. Across the mental health disciplines, certain professional associations continue to pursue similar outmoded efforts, presumably in the name of ethics.

There is some logic for allowing professional associations, which have intimate familiarity with the disciplines and a commitment to public welfare, to provide some structuring of promotional efforts, such as (perhaps) guidelines for advertising. Nevertheless, public policy has moved away from allowing professional ethics committees primary policing power over errant practitioners. Instead, public policy now favors recourse to regulatory agencies and courts of law. In fact, public policy now seems to reflect a certain distrust of the underlying motives of professional associations that promulgate ethical guidelines related to promotion and advertising: "The Federal Trade Commission, after a year and a half of discussion and negotiation with the American Psychological Association, has demanded that the association abolish those sections of its ethical principles that prohibit fee-splitting and some kinds of advertising. The commission says such prohibitions constitute unfair restraint of trade" (Bales, 1988, p. 19). Bales also reports that the FTC is concerned about prohibitions against clients' testimonials about quality of service, against advertisements of unique or one-of-a-kind abilities, against advertisements that appeal to fears or anxiety, and against other kinds of promotional activity, including statements about the comparative desirability of services, direct solicitations of individual clients, the giving or receiving of compensation for referrals, and the offering of services directly to someone who is already receiving similar services from another professional. While this particular dispute is still unresolved, it points toward the distinctly opposing views of professional associations and the new public policy.

Promotional Communication

In the context of marketing, public communications are directed at promoting a professional service, with their purpose being "to educate, persuade, inform, or remind the target market about various aspects of [one's] services" (Forman and Forman, 1987, p. 84). Forman and Forman also identify "four basic types of promotional channels: sales promotion, personal selling, publicity, and advertising" (p. 85). Keep in mind that promotional methods include but are not limited to advertising itself. While advertising provides a useful method for illustrating the principles of promotion, other methods can also be promotional: public speaking, mental health information for clients, and professional writing and research (selected promotional strategies will be discussed in detail later in this chapter).

Decisions about promotional communication will be based on the marketing analysis and objectives and on the practical limitations of the budget. At this point, however, it is sufficient to say that a *tentative budget mix* must be developed early; that is, a tentative idea must be formed about how budget allocations will be made for the different communication options that are being considered for selection (Ray, 1982). (More will be said later about promotional resource allocation.)

The promotional plan for mental health services aims to inform prospective clients about the mental health practice and includes both directional and intrusive communications (Walker 1979). *Directional communications* assume that the potential client accepts the need for mental health services and is seeking the proper professional to meet that need. Thus, the desire to acquire or purchase service already exists; the potential client is apt to consider alternative service sources, and the promotional communication seeks to tell him or her all that is needed (or at least enough to whet the purchasing appetite) and to create an attraction to the particular mental health practice. Since it is educational, directional communication is probably the most palatable to mental health professionals.

Intrusive communications unabashedly but tactfully invade the potential client's privacy with a message that may or may not be needed, expected, or even wanted. In other words, the message is imposed through a selected medium, such as radio, where a commercial interrupts a musical program. Tradition-bound professionals may be quick to criticize intrusive advertising, however. For example, one mental health practitioner advertised his availability in a legal newspaper, but a letter to the editor alleged that such an announcement suggested that attorneys had a special need for mental health services. The correspondent expressed resentment of the perceived connotation of mental illness among attorneys. In another example, a marriage and family therapist advertised on a radio station, saying that divorce could perhaps be avoided by counseling, but another mental health practitioner called the station manager and said that the advertisement was in poor taste and that it promoted divorce.

Promotional communications contribute to the marketing and public relations functions. According to Mahon (1978), the broad marketing and public relations objectives include retaining current clients, gaining new ones, expanding the use of services, and fostering social involvement. These objectives must be supported by a strong organizational structure, adequate geographical coverage, a complete service line, high technical competence and quality, specialized disciplinary expertise, a competitive fee structure, high employee morale, and unassailable ethical standards. Then and only then can promotional communications be selected from the available media and formats, such as speeches and other oral communications, publications, and press releases, announcements, or articles.

It is important to tailor a promotional message (especially related to mental health care) for as wide a range of idiosyncratic receiving processes as possible. This is because people wish to avoid messages that challenge their basic beliefs, and any message received must be processed for memory and recall (Ray, 1982). Every person has certain limitations on his or her ability to process information and typically preserves only a minor portion of a promotional message.

Do-It-Yourself Versus Advertising Agents

Promotional communications require special expertise, yet the mental health CEO may be prone to adopt a do-it-yourself approach. As with accounting and legal services, the mental health professional can assimilate only so much knowledge and can develop only limited technical skills in areas where he or she has had little or no formal training. Entrepreneurship involves personal commitment to making a project successful, but foolhardy and wasteful efforts have no place. Therefore, one's promotional communications should be the best available for one's task and resources.

Without specialized training in marketing, the mental health entrepreneur may be prey to erroneous ideas about marketing. For example, one mental health CEO mailed over seven thousand copies of a brochure about her practice to a wide variety of potential referral sources in the community. She was disappointed when there was not a single immediate referral that could be attributed to the brochure. She reasoned that since mailed brochures had a reasonably solid record of gaining enrollments for professional seminars (some sources have estimated a 7 percent enrollment rate for a well-planned seminar project), they should also do well in attracting therapy clients. Had she been more familiar with marketing, she would have known that the types of persons who respond to advertising for professional seminars have quite different objectives from those of people who seek therapy, and that when a brochure for clinical services is mailed to a potential referral source, it is most effective when a personalized contact follows (by telephone or in person). (Of course, her mailing of the brochures may yield a long-term payoff in the form of enhanced organizational image in the professional service community.)

An alternative to the do-it-yourself approach is to obtain

the services of a public relations or advertising agency. According to Ray (1982, pp. 24–25), "There are nearly four thousand advertising agencies listed in the *Standard Directory of Advertising Agencies* in the United States. The same directory lists only about fifty sales promotion agencies. Advertising agencies range in size from the giant J. Walter Thompson Company (which annually spends the equivalent of $1.5 billion worth of advertising) to the newest small agency (which has a staff consisting of one person who does writing and graphics work for advertising, sales promotion, or publicity)." Generally, these agencies offer assistance with all aspects of the communication mix, perhaps including research and graphic production. They may provide direct service, arrange for contracts for service, or consult with the mental health CEO about obtaining services elsewhere. Above all, an advertising agency can create and place advertisements in a way that will help the mental health organization achieve its communications and sales objectives.

Compensation for advertising agencies varies, but it commonly involves a commission (such as 15 percent of the cost for an advertisement). Thus, if an advertising agency placed a $1,000 advertisement in a local newspaper, it would receive $150. There is also a noncommission system, which may involve markups on materials purchased or contractual agreements to replace or augment commissions.

The mental health CEO should not lightly rule out the use of an advertising agency because of costs. In the long run, an inept do-it-yourself plan may prove more costly than an investment in professionally produced advertising. Besides the technical skills and contacts necessary to get the job done efficiently and effectively, the advertising agency can offer an objective and professional perspective on the strengths and weaknesses endemic to the particular mental health practice group: "Management should realize that the strength of having an outside agency is the potential for powerful new ideas to occur. The outside agency brings the outside point of view and allows unusual or marginal types to bring free thinking to bear on communication problems" (Ray, 1982, p. 77). Free thinking is indispensable for solving problems in mental health entrepreneurship.

Determining the Promotional Campaign

An effective promotional campaign never involves only a single effort, strategy, or technique (such as an advertisement in the yellow pages of a telephone directory); it is an ongoing process that involves multiple promotional vehicles. Effective marketing does not happen quickly or on a once-and-for-all basis. There will be analysis, implementation, research on effects, possibly some trial and error, reformulations, and on and on. The effects of one marketing venture may not become evident until much later, and the intervening marketing changes will confound the evaluative data—such is the nature of promotional strategies. To put it simply, the promotional campaign must continue throughout the operation of the mental health business, and its course must be altered repeatedly to maximize the campaign's benefits.

Resource Allocation. It would be nice if a mental health CEO could implement the ideal promotional system. Unfortunately, the nebulous nature of data derived from market analysis makes determination of such an ideal system a will-o'-the-wisp goal, and the hard core of financial reality may block implementation of the CEO's preferred approach.

The mental health CEO must decide how resources will be allocated, and the best guideline is probably "getting the most bang for the buck." As Ray (1982, p. 38) says, one "keep[s] allocating resources to aspects of the mix until the extra response [one gets] is equal to the extra expenditure for the element of the mix." This is termed the *marginal economic approach.* It is seldom possible, however, to achieve this approach with confidence. Although the mental health CEO may have some experience with or a preference for certain elements of the promotional mix, the mental health organization may be forced (such as by a national disciplinary code of ethics) to avoid certain strategies or to be aligned with a particular medium or element. Other shaping influences may come from community attitudes, the habits of professional counterparts in the area, and the preferences of the mental health professionals and support staff members in the practice group.

There is no one formula for deciding how much money should be allocated to promotional communications, or how the fund should be subdivided to cover different segments of the promotional mix. One guideline, which may be based more on folklore than on scientific reasoning, holds that 5 percent of the gross income should be reinvested into promoting the professional practice. That is an easy-to-understand and seemingly reasonable idea; logically, however it may fall short, because the percentage of gross income could justifiably be varied according to the developmental stage or special goals of the mental health practice.

There are several ways to determine the promotional budget. Mental health professionals tend to be very conservative with marketing dollars; they always seem to figure that their academic qualifications and years of experience will bring clients to their doorsteps. While this may or may not have been true in days gone by, it is certainly not true in today's mental health industry. In a somewhat sermonizing way, Walker (1979, pp. 54–55) talks to professionals about their relying on four approaches to funding promotional communications:

> 1. The *"I'll spend what I can afford"* approach. Spending only what you think you can afford treats advertising as a luxury—an indulgence. This attitude reflects an underlying feeling that you really don't consider it a serious means of marketing your services. Subconsciously, you may look at commercials as wasters of dollars. In that case, you probably shouldn't be advertising at all.
>
> 2. The *"I'll match the competition"* approach. Because your colleague across the street runs a weekly six-inch, two-column ad in the local shopper, your inclination might be to do something of the same. Fight off the impulse. This is a purely defensive approach rather than an aggressive one. It's better to make a careful analysis of the audience

you wish to contact and what you want to accomplish instead of blindly imitating your competitor.

3. The *"I'll invest a percentage of gross income"* approach. This more forward-looking attitude makes two constructive assumptions: (a) advertising is an investment for a larger future return, and (b) a scientific formula is necessary to figure the budget allocation.

A percentage of annual income will automatically have you taking for granted that advertising promotes the sale of services. It recognizes commercial communication as an important contributor to the expansion of a professional practice. The only danger is that your allocation based on last year's figures may be too optimistic for this year. A business cycle could dip and pull down your sale of services. Then, when advertising is necessary even more than before, you feel the need to cut back on funds.

4. The *"I'll allocate so much per head"* approach. A variation of the percentage-of-gross-income method is the *unit-of-sales* approach. According to the number of new clients or patients that entered your practice last year, you designate a minimum value per head [p. 55].

Walker indicates that the fourth approach is the one most likely to generate profits.

With a bit more academic objectivity, Braun (1981) describes four methods for determining promotional expenditures. The *task method* is based on what is to be accomplished and what is necessary to accomplish the objectives. There is never enough money, of course, to ensure fulfillment of the objectives, and so this must be a calculated, "best-we-can-do" decision. The *percentage of gross income method* relies on a percentage (as discussed previously). A fraction of gross income— say, 1 percent to over 15 percent, depending on business needs, objectives, and resources—can be assigned to paying for promotional communications. The *empirical method* applies experimental procedures to determine the budget. These include tests of creative appeal and media mix; since marketing conditions change constantly, research must be continual. The *media requirement method* allows the budget to be determined according to the amount of media coverage necessary to communicate with a predetermined number of potential clients. Whatever amount of money is allocated to promotional communication, the sum should be derived from a careful marketing analysis and be consonant with the business plan.

Selecting Promotional Strategies. The promotional campaign will reflect the critical decision of which medium or media will be used for particular promotional communications. The mental health CEO must know how consumers are likely to react to the flood of communications that inundates them daily: "Every day, the average American is exposed to 1,000 commercial messages—from 8,600 radio stations, 725 TV stations, 9,500 newspapers, and 9,800 magazines and professional and business publications" (Braun, 1981, p. 13).

Consumers apparently favor promotional communications that provide information about a professional's qualifications and specialties and allow them to make comparisons between that practitioner and others. To discover the type of message that elicits a favorable response, an in-office questionnaire, a telephone survey, or a mail survey may yield useful data for planning promotional communications. Braun (1981) cautions that the request for information must be clearly delineated: too much must not be asked, the request must be short, and respondent should be told how their cooperation will be beneficial to themselves and others.

The desired market position should provide a framework for selecting the promotional strategy. Of course, the results of promotional communications that are based on a chosen market position can lead to repositioning (expanding, reducing, or changing the market sector). Positioning or repositioning must be based on research and facts. It should set short- and long-term goals, hold to a budget, select a medium (or media), create a message (or messages), and evaluate outcomes.

Once positioning is temporarily determined, the next step is to make a decision about media. Ray (1982, pp. 382–383) provides four guidelines:

> 1. The large number of alternative media and vehicles should be narrowed down on the basis of qualitative analysis stemming from consumer and creative considerations . . . .
> 2. The alternative vehicle types should be compared on the basis of audience composition at the vehicle exposure level. It is important to get media that are efficient in terms of reaching target segments. The data from audience studies are available and good enough for making rough cuts suggested at this stage.
> 3. The planner should make some assessment of advertising exposure for each medium and general class of vehicle. If there is reason to believe that particular vehicle types would not produce a great proportion of advertising exposure among the vehicle exposure audience, then these vehicles should be dropped from consideration or certainly put in a lower-consideration class. The assessment of advertising exposure can be made on the basis of individual company and media studies (combined with judgment about the ability of the medium or vehicle to lead to advertising exposure) . . . .
> 4. Finally, some assessment should be made of the proportion of individuals who will reach some level of advertising communication as defined by the objectives of the campaign . . . . In each situation, the media planner makes some assessment of the conversion proportion from audience to advertising exposure to advertising communication.

The mental health CEO can select from the following types of media and their vehicles:

> *Print advertising:* Newspapers, magazines, supplements.

Mail advertising: Newsletters, personal letters, direct-response mailings, postcard reminders.

Printed matter: Brochures, folders, booklets, stuffers.

Signs and transit advertising: Indoor signs, outdoor signs, billboards, transportation posters, spectaculars.

Broadcast advertising: Radio—AM and FM; TV—VHF and UHF; public broadcasting stations; cable TV [Braun, 1981, p. 17].

(A later section will discuss the special relevance of certain media and vehicles to the promotion of mental health services.)

In making decisions for the promotional campaign and selecting the promotional strategies in particular, the mental health CEO should determine *what* should be said to the designated market sector (this is known as *message positioning*). Achieving the goal of appealing to the potential clients depends on the decision of *how* to say it (otherwise known as the *format*). Creative philosophies enter into perceptual mapping: "The attitudinal framework for message positioning would suggest that three more bits of information are necessary. First, we must learn the ideal point and acceptable range of values for each characteristic . . . . The second bit of information we need for message positioning is how the consumer uses the characteristics . . . . We need to know how consumers position our brand and others on the market. Once the characteristics, ideal points and acceptable ranges, decision process, and brand perceptions are known, a framework for message positioning is complete" (Ray, 1982, pp. 44–45). As might be assumed, before actual marketing expenditures are made, one must develop the information for the positioning framework and strategies for changing characteristics, perceptions, and options for promotional communications. So far, the process is still at the stage of situational analysis.

The creative-artistic dimension of marketing is manifested in the *message format*. The decision on form is best reached through a marketing-communication research effort, consisting of seven steps: problem formation (structure); behavioral analysis (what has and has not worked in the past); alternative solutions (generating options); pretesting (format alternatives); computer simulation, if feasible; field experimentation (test marketing); and campaign marketing (continuing the promotional communications research on success and failure in achieving objectives and goals) (Ray, 1982). The message format is then applied to a *message distribution plan.* Earlier marketing steps have narrowed down the choices: "On the basis of past experience, budgetary restraints, type of communication goal and audience, the nature of the appeals and format, and pretesting results—many media, vehicles, and schedules have been eliminated from consideration" (Ray, 1982, p. 48).

When the market communication plan is implemented, there must be continual *budget control.* Careful financial control helps determine the effectiveness of the campaign and provides data for making decisions about changes or other actions, as necessary (for example, understanding and assessing possible future strategies). Consequently, information-gathering procedures must be selected. These can range from simply asking new clients why they chose a particular mental health practice group to conducting a rigorous investigation of many subjects.

Formulating the Promotional Message

The preferred and most effective message(s) will be idiosyncratic and depend on the type of professional service, the qualities of the mental health practice and the characteristics of its professionals, the attitudes and needs of the community and market sectors, and timing. In other words, nothing is fixed for determining the message, and—as in virtually every other aspect of marketing—continued evaluation and reformulation are necessary. There are, however, some general guidelines.

To achieve a positive client response, Walker (1979, p. 88) suggests five guidelines:

1. Your advertising must be *consistent* if it is to attract the attention of present clients or patients, and reach new ones.

2. It must *create and stimulate a desire* for people to purchase your special kind of service.
3. It must offer the consumer a *real dollar value*— exceedingly important for adding new buyers to build volume.
4. The advertising must *convince* readers, listeners, or viewers beyond the shadow of a doubt that they can obtain *quality services* and that their *satisfaction* is the most important object for you.
5. Every professional service ad you run must project such a favorable image to the client or patient that he or she will make a special effort to have only *you* be the purveyor of those services [emphasis in original].

In professional services, it is especially important for the actual professional (not an actor or an employee) to be part of the promotional communication. This may consume the professional's time, but it is an important aid to effective marketing. For example, indications are that there may well be benefits to the professional answering his or her own office telephone whenever possible, instead of using an intermediary (a receptionist). Many clients have reported pleasure from the ease of (at least some of the time) getting a direct and immediate response from the professional. ("After all, I was not calling to talk to a secretary!")

Whatever the medium or vehicle may be, the promotional communication must attract the receiver (client). For professional mental health services, successful promotional communication should embrace "the six A's" (Forman and Forman, 1987): The client must become aware of the *availability* of the service and the particular mental health practitioner; the mental health services must be *accessible*, such as by prompt appointments (return telephone calls immediately); the services must be *affordable*, at least to the targeted market sector; the *ability* or standard of care must be unquestionable; a positive *appearance* or image of the mental health organization and its professionals and support staff members should be depicted; and, since no client prefers to deal with an unpleasant practitioner, the representation of the professional must convey *affability*, as relevant to the conditions, such as empathic understanding, that promote a helping relationship.

The framing of the promotional communication should also aim to achieve "the four R's of advertising" (Walker, 1979, p. 56):

1. *REACH*—the determination of your market.
2. *READERSHIP* (or listeners or viewers)—the people who are really interested in what you have to offer.
3. *RETENTION*—the number of those who remember your message after they have seen it.
4. *RESULTS*—the selling power of what you've said and its ability to provide a return for investment.

The best plans for reach, readership, and retention are to no avail unless there are results relevant to the organizational objectives. Walker (1979, p. 62) suggests that the results can be detected in "(1) *awareness* by clients or patients that your services are available, (2) *knowledge* by clients or patients that there are certain advantages in making use of these services, and (3) *belief* by clients or patients that your time and attention offer the best value for the prices quoted." Attainment of results will depend on *believability*, which requires starting with the truth, appealing to the main desires of the targeted market sector, giving a reasonable explanation to justify clients' belief, and using clear and descriptive language.

The concept of fair competition imposes two criteria for all promotional communications. The information must be honest and accurate (no false representations), and the message must not produce misleading impressions (no subterfuge). In commercial sales, these two criteria can be met and yet "puffing" or touting the product will still be acceptable. In mental health service, "puffing" is not acceptable. The mental health promotional communication can appropriately describe the qualities of services and practitioners, even conveying their superiority over competitors (if that is true), but the message should not "puff," for two reasons. First, typical consumer-clients still prefer professional services to be justified by dignified factual assertions (since clients' personal welfare, rather than just the price of a product, is at stake), and "puffing" may alienate many potential clients. Second, risk management contraindicates the issuing of any message that could reasonably be interpreted as a guarantee of treatment outcomes or of an unusually high standard of care (see Chapter Eight, this volume; Woody, 1988a).

With the foregoing in mind, the do-it-yourself mental health CEO should consider the following advice (Adams, 1965, p. 35):

> Before you pick up a pencil, pick up the facts. Detachment is fine, but ignorance is inexcusable.
> First make sure you have something to say that is worth saying. Then communicate it in a way that people can understand. Remember that too much creativity can often obscure a good message.
> Make certain that you are neither insulting your prospect's intelligence nor offending his judgment. Remember that it's better to impress a small audience than to offend a large one.
> Following the new leaders is just as dangerous as following the old leaders. Imitation may be the sincerest form of flattery, but in advertising, it can also be the shortest route to disaster.
> Make sure that the principal thought in your advertising appeals to a human emotion . . . . Then use your talent and ingenuity to present that thought in the most intriguing and provocative way. Try to be different, but first try to be good!
> You must train yourself to communicate with people on their level, not yours. When a reader decides to look at your ad, he gives you a slice out

of his life. You had better reward him by talking
to him in his language. One nod from a customer
is worth two awards on the wall.

These ideas have special relevance for mental health professionals. If he or she is not careful, the professional may lace an advertisement with terms or "psychobabble" that will obscure the
message, be too intellectual, imply the reader's pathology, or
provoke defensiveness. A message may also create a positive
feeling about the benefits of treatment, but only if there is a humane, "everyday folks" style of delivery. A message like
"Everyone sometimes experiences ups and downs, and therapy
can help you get rid of the downside" says, "You are not devi-
ant or sick, and together we can improve the situation and the
future can be better." In contrast, a message like "Depression
can plague your health and career, but therapy can modify your
adverse emotions and behavioral maladaptions" is geared toward
a different intellectual level and perceptual set.

If there is one common fault among mental health professionals who attempt to do their own marketing, it is that
they use too many words. A bit of reason will usually shed
some light on how intellectual the message should be for a targeted market sector. As an expert, the professional has deep intellectual insight into issues. In presenting a promotional communication, his or her tendency is to explain the issue too fully
(for example, describing psychotherapy in process terms, with
reference to theoretical or technical concepts, while clients simply want to know what is expected of them personally and financially and what it will take to get relief from their problems).
As a general rule, review every draft of a promotional communication to eliminate words and simplify language. There is no
one best way to formulate a message: "There is no formula for
making successful promotional materials. What works in one
market may not work in another market. By the same token,
one segment's positive response is no indicator of the response
another will have. The only way to know for certain is to test
your materials" (Forman and Forman, 1987, p. 109). With that
caveat, there is a five-step procedure for developing the message

format (Ray, 1982). First, have a clear definition of the problem (idea development). Second, carefully review available knowledge about the types of formats that can be used. Third, generate specific alternatives, moving from rough to finished versions. Fourth, pretest (or at least critically examine) specific alternatives (the decision stage). Fifth, distribute the message. In formulating the problem, attention is given to the target market (influencing characteristics), the appeal or positioning of the campaign (the difficulties of reaching the market), the competition (what major competitors do, the noise and clutter in the communication environment), the tone of the message (refutational, argumentative), and the rationale (how the components of the message work together to obtain the objectives). Although this almost goes without saying, perhaps a sixth step should be added: The distributed message is always subject to appraisal and revision.

Selected Mental Health Promotional Strategies

There is no one definitive approach to promoting mental health services. Moreover, the nature of marketing, combined with the idiosyncratic aspects of mental health services, leave the mental health CEO with few objective data on which to base decisions about communications media or vehicles. Unless he or she has had extensive training or experience in health-care marketing, the mental health professional may harbor numerous misconceptions about advertising. The following sections present ideas and recommendations derived from the experience, successes, and failures of many mental health CEOs.

Business Cards, Announcements, Signs, and Letterhead Stationery. One of the greatest misconceptions among mental health professionals is that a business card, an announcement of a practice's opening, a sign, or letterhead stationery will bring in business. In fact, there seems to be little of actual promotional value in these vehicles; basically, they are for informational purposes, to help someone know how to make contact with the practitioner. Occasionally the announcement of a practice's opening will prompt another professional to make a courtesy referral, but this is rare. Signs, too, seldom do more than help someone already looking for the office locate it. Likewise, there is little (if any) research to document that an expensive, distinctive letterhead will generate more referrals or create a more positive image than a less expensive, undistinctive letterhead will. (One survey did find that plastic business cards are kept more often than paper ones are.) Vendors who sell and promote these materials stand to make a profit, and while these vehicles may be productive for other types of businesses, whether they offer benefits to a mental health practice remains questionable. To be sure, these vehicles are important for conveying an image of the mental health service. Therefore, they can offer a positive communication force, but they cannot be expected to generate business. More often than not, the mental health practitioner spends too much money on business cards, announcements, signs, and letterhead stationery, while the money would be better spent (especially in the early days of the practice) on more effective promotional communications. Why, then, is so much priority placed on getting impressive letterhead stationery? Even among mental health professionals, vanity can rear its ugly head.

Image Building. A common concern of all mental health promotional vehicles or strategies is to build an awareness of and respect for the mental health practice and its professionals. The goal is to cultivate and implant a positive image in the minds of potential clients and referral sources. Personal contact, mass media, and all other promotional strategies should contribute to this goal.

Mental health practitioners pursue diverse life-styles, but effective marketing requires any practitioner to gear his or her actions toward constructing a positive professional image. One's personal activities affect one's professional image. Driving an expensive automobile or being a fashion plate may promote self-aggrandizement more than a positive image. If one prefers and can afford expensive automobiles and clothing, fine; but they are not essential to promoting the business. Instead, the emphasis should be on conduct that reflects intellectual and academic stature and supports honorable social values. Abuse of any substance (including alcohol and tobacco), lack of physical fitness, and antisocial or sociopathic behavior contradict a holistic health-care model and may have a negative impact on the practitioner's business. One's personal life-style and conduct can be a powerful promotional vehicle.

It seems that the best single promotional approach is to build a strong professional and personal image in the community that contains one's targeted market sector. Simply getting one's name known around town is insufficient; it is also necessary to earn respect. Perhaps the best source of respect will be one's former clients. There is nothing quite so convincing as a satisfied customer, and care should be taken to ensure that after their therapy has ended, clients will have a positive view of it and know that the mental health practitioner will appreciate their making referrals in the future. Others in the community— laypersons and professionals alike who have adequate knowledge of the mental health practitioner's competence and characteristics—will also be able, even without having personally received treatment, to make persuasive recommendations.

Personal Contact with Referral Sources. Personal contact with a potential referral source is an excellent promotional option. When it comes to mental health services, clients want the assurance that their well-being is in good hands, and a respected person's or organization's endorsement encourages prospective clients to inquire about and accept a mental health practitioner's services.

When an announcement or a brochure is mailed, a follow-up personal contact by telephone or in person is helpful (and probably essential to acquiring a referral). Sometimes a small but relevant gift (for example, a book written by the practitioner or describing his or her type of service) is appropriate and motivates another professional to make a referral. In making contact with another professional, the practitioner should consider what the prospective source can gain from making a referral: Contact with other mental health professionals may enhance public relations but do little in terms of promotional benefit, while contact with attorneys or physicians may provide them an opportunity to enhance their quality and standard of care.

The two-martini lunch is unlikely to elicit referrals. This is not to say that a "working lunch" is never useful for promotional purposes; many practitioners advocate this method. When a meeting of this nature is productive, however, it is usually because it provides a personal link and a chance to learn about each other's qualifications. One will not impress referral sources by wining and dining them. A certain amount of socializing may be fine, but extensive time spent at lunch with prospective sources is inefficient.

Personal Contact with Consumer Groups. Although it takes time, public speaking generates an important image for the mental health group practice, educates consumers (thereby creating a need), and elicits inquiries from possible clients. Speaking to groups known to have a connection with the specific type of services one offers is logical; for example, practitioners who serve children and their families should certainly reach out to school-related groups. This is a slow but reasonably sure way of developing a mental health practice.

Professional Networks. A professional network should produce reciprocal benefits. If another professional makes a referral, the mental health CEO should try to send a referral in return. Obviously, the wish to reciprocate cannot outweigh good judgment; if the referral is undeserved or would not be in the best interest of the client, one should not make it.

A network can reach well beyond one's immediate locale. Leadership activities in professional associations and the publication of books and articles can acquaint professionals elsewhere with the practitioners in a group. When one has an opportunity to communicate with a nationally prominent group of professionals, one should tactfully use promotional materials— for example, putting reference materials on letterhead stationery instead of on plain paper, enclosing a copy of one's brochure, and so on. Many marketers say that the best single way to build a national (and local) professional network is to send a hand-written note of thanks for even the most minimal favors, perhaps followed up by a nominal gift ("Here's a copy of an article in which I thought you might be interested"). Whenever one engages in a noteworthy professional activity (for example, publishing an article or a book, delivering a paper at a conference, being elected to an office, serving on a committee for a professional association), one should issue a press release to the local mass media.

Mass Media. Many of the same benefits available from personal contact with community referral sources, consumer groups, and professional networks can also be gained through the use of mass media. If advertisements are purchased, exposure can be quite expensive. At the same time, a mass medium can reach a large number of potential consumers, and if a message is tailored to the medium's known audience, it can produce immediate results. One practitioner reported, "For every dollar that I spend on a radio advertisement, I make ten dollars—to me that's a reasonable expenditure to attract new clients." The mass media typically require specialized expertise for the preparation of promotional messages, which adds to production costs.

A true marketing windfall awaits the mental health CEO who can engineer free publicity. Most radio and television stations have an obligation to air public service messages, and most newspapers and magazines are always open to material with human interest or welfare information. For this kind of exposure, emphasizing the health-care thrust and downplaying the direct solicitation of clients can persuade a programming executive or an editor to transmit a message for the sake of public education. If time and money are at a premium, which is usually the case, priority should be given to public information via the mass media. At the same time, this can be a competitive area; it seems as if every mental health practitioner aspires to write an Ann Landers–type of column for the local newspaper.

Mental health professionals traditionally have relied on advertising in the print media (newspapers, magazines, and particularly the yellow pages of the telephone directory). This reliance has probably been due to their ability to control the dignity of the advertisements, as dictated specifically by professional codes of ethics. Today, there is an expanding array of advertising vehicles, and heavy reliance on advertisements in the print media should be reevaluated.

In general, the print media can pay dividends, but marketing analysis must pinpoint positive and negative factors. The print media have been used often in the past by the professions, but that is no reason to limit one's marketing efforts and promotional funds to them; the probability of actual promotional benefits should be assessed objectively.

Agents for different kinds of advertising tout their payoffs, but there is reason to doubt that a printed advertisement is any more effective in bringing in the right kind of client than another promotional option. For example, one practitioner reported that he advertised in the business section of his local newspaper, hoping to draw affluent executives. After several weeks of regular advertisements, he received two self-referred clients, both of whom proved to be sociopathic and refused to pay for service. A marriage and family therapist's print ads produced nothing but inquiries from persons who could not afford to pay for service. Beyond a listing or a minimal advertisement for identification purposes, it is doubtful that the larger and more expensive advertisements in the yellow pages bring in adequate numbers of clients with the ability to pay for service. Locales and market sectors may, however, differ substantially in their responses to print advertisements. Most print advertising sources have conducted detailed market analyses. The practitioner should study these data carefully and remember that these sources, too, may "puff" their services or transmit only positive information to influence potential advertisers.

Educational Materials. Closely akin to public education via the mass media, a worthwhile promotional strategy is to prepare short and simple educational messages about emotional and behavioral problems and the alternative treatments that are available. In this age of desktop publishing, it is relatively easy and inexpensive to produce first-class articles or manuals that will be

perceived as valued gifts. These can be widely distributed at
health fairs (commonly sponsored by hospitals or health-care
associations), by social agencies and health-care facilities, or in
medical and legal offices. Direct solicitation should be minimal; the emphasis should be on high standards and on the benefits of treatment. The message should be informative and up-
beat, with attainable rewards highlighted but not guaranteed. A
footnote can contain a statement of the practitioner's qualifications, name, and address, as well as a telephone number for
follow-up information about professional services.

The Service Brochure. One of the most used and most abused
promotional vehicles is the service brochure. Almost every mental health practitioner has some sort of handout about his or
her practice, but seldom does this handout fulfill its potential,
either for promotion or for risk management. Indeed, the great
majority of such handouts fail, their cost and slick appearance
notwithstanding (Moldenhauer, 1987/88).

Since every service brochure should be tailored to the situation, no model is offered here. Suffice it to say that "every
written document disseminated to clients should be tailored to
the qualifications, standards, competencies, and priorities of the
particular professional/service and to the characteristics of the
targets (that is, the type of clientele that is to be attracted and
served)" (Woody, 1988b, p. 89). Successful service brochures
have the following characteristics:

> Their underlying strategy is lucid, clearly present-
> ing specific benefits of the service. Their benefits
> are made concrete, backed with data or case his-
> tories, and are distinguished from the competition
> by being specific. The brochure itself is easily
> scanned and read . . . . Their quality and content
> make a strong impression on the reader. Not only
> are the graphics compelling, but the words and vi-
> suals work together to reinforce a unique message.
> The current communications glut puts pressure on
> short, punchy copy and bold graphics. Paper and

printing must be high quality to communicate design and content.

Their purpose is to work with other elements in the marketing mix. Their style or approach matches the people selling and providing the service, and may be the first step in the sales presentation which is delivered on a one-to-one basis. Remember the key to providing further service is people [Moldenhauer, 1987/88, p. 126].

Rubright and MacDonald (1981) offer guidelines for information that the service brochure should include. It should discuss the following:

- Organizational purposes and mission statement
- Services offered
- Benefits (documented by research or testimonials, if possible)
- A supportive referral network
- How to make initial contact for service
- Who will be the initial contact, and what will be the intake procedure
- What kind of clientele uses the services
- Typical treatment scenarios (number of appointments, waiting periods)
- Payment arrangements (credit, cash, credit cards, third-party payers, sliding fee scale, gratis service)
- Scheduling details (days and hours for service) and emergency provisions
- Alternatives after service ends (routine follow-up, referrals)
- The roster of associated professionals (qualifications, special licensures/certifications)
- Management issues (supervision)
- Location of service sites
- Affiliation with other organizations or practitioners
- Relations with other community services
- Certifications and accreditations (if any) of the practice group

- Memberships in significant organizations (United Way, HMOs, and so on).

Obviously, some of these topics will have little or no relevance for a particular practice group. Whatever its contents or format, however, the language of the service brochure must be clear and geared to the comprehension level of most potential clients. To accomplish its promotional and risk-management objectives, the service brochure should also include a message that emphasizes the service's personal attention, high-quality care, and affordability (with a "hook" to prompt the reader to take immediate action).

The service brochure serves several purposes. It prevents clients' misperceptions about, for example, qualifications or guarantees of "cure." It creates needs in clients via information and personal connection. It establishes a quasi-contractual framework for those who later receive service. Most of all, it motivates potential clients to step forward, at least for more information (that is, more promotional communication) and, preferably, for trial service.

Some mental health CEOs have found it economical to respond to inquiries (as opposed to distinct referrals) by saying, "Why don't you come in for a no-charge session? I can learn more about your situation and help you decide whether our clinic is the best place for your treatment." Although this approach requires investing a whole session in a potential client, it should be thought of as investing money in a promotional strategy. If one free session leads to ten or more that are paid for, it may be a wise investment of time. Indeed, an informal survey shows that very few such sessions remain one-time-only encounters, especially if the offer of a free session is made only to those who seem seriously interested in service. Whenever there is an inquiry, even from someone who seems only slightly interested, the routine should be to record the inquirer's name and address, send a service brochure, and possibly follow up a short time later ("I wanted to let you know that I appreciated your inquiry a couple of weeks ago, and I wondered if you had any other questions").

This review of selected mental health promotional strategies has emphasized that there can be no blanket endorsement or condemnation of any medium, format, vehicle, or strategy. Every promotional decision must be based on market research unique to the mental health practice. The primary guideline for success in mental health practice is this: Planning, developing, selecting, implementing, evaluating, and revising promotional strategies is a major responsibility of the mental health CEO, and no success is possible without astute promotional communications.

CHAPTER 5

Guidelines for Forming a Practice Group

WHEN IT COMES TIME TO FORM A MENTAL HEALTH practice group, traditional professionalism can be a shibboleth for business planning and decision making. Many professionals buy into the notion of blanket equality among colleagues, when there may in fact be gross differences in competence. The sound practitioner makes a judgment about rights within the practice group on the basis of each colleague's contribution or investment. An affiliation among mental health professionals must be based on commercial considerations and sound reasoning, not on any presumptions birthed in a bygone era or from nonbusiness parentage.

At least some decisions about defining the practice (for example, specifying the services that will be provided), business planning, and marketing decisions should occur before one even thinks about an affiliation with others. Experience reveals that the sequence for decisions about these matters is often confused. Consider the following two examples.

First, new graduates who cannot find employment decide to pool their resources and open a private practice together, reasoning, "We have had several graduate classes together and have always enjoyed one another's company." But a business perspective demands the question "Will we mutually benefit from one another's company?" Second, several mental health professionals who have worked together in a facility conclude that their salaried positions relegate them to a dead-end financial path, and they decide to travel together in clinical practice, knowing one another only within the confines of their institutional roles. By the time that these mental health professionals seek legal or accounting advice, they have already agreed on one thing: They will affiliate. Often they have agreed on all sorts of other issues, such as ownership rights and duties, without adequate information about the legal and financial implications. By this point, it is almost always too late to do any meaningful definition of practice, business planning, or marketing analysis that could complement the other decisions.

These examples prompt a definite recommendation: Don't put the cart before the horse. The temptation to cement affiliations without a thorough understanding of the issues, especially legal liability and financial implications, can jeopardize the principals and their families. For example, if the practitioner is emotionally upset by a bad affiliation, family relations will suffer; if money is wasted on a poor venture, funds for the children's college education may needlessly go down the drain. More often than not, professionals make quick decisions on who is going to be part of a group out of personal urgency to feel progress toward improving their careers and thereby dissipating anxiety and insecurity. Such premature decisions, spurred by emotional needs, are likely to provide only false assurances and may usher in profound disruptive anxiety and real reasons for being insecure. The professional with a tendency to rush headlong into an affiliation (or any other sort of decision) might consider the wisdom of tempering that urge.

In deference to the prevailing (even if erroneous) sequence of decisions, this chapter considers (1) how to select professional affiliates, (2) the structural form for a clinical practice (including legal business entities), (3) important conditions that should be spelled out contractually (the fiduciary relationship, financial obligations, specific duties and compensations, noncompetition, and indemnification), (4) using important allies (notably an accountant and an attorney), and (5) group dynamics.

Selecting Professional Affiliates

A decision to affiliate with another professional cannot be predicated only on mutual liking. This attraction is defined by the concept of similarity: There is a natural human tendency to be attracted to someone like ourselves. According to Michener, DeLamater, and Schwartz (1986, p. 331), "On the whole, evidence indicates that birds of a feather *do* flock together; we are attracted to people who are like ourselves." Attitude similarity (sharing of beliefs, opinions, likes, and dislikes) is an important form of attraction.

Attraction and Cognitive Consistency. The underlying reason for attraction is that people have a desire for cognitive consistency—that is, internal dissonance or uneasiness is provoked by contact or interaction with someone who does not agree with us or who disputes our preferred attitudes. Consequently, we tend to avoid persons with dissimilar attitudes, and we "flock together" with persons who, when we interact with them, validate our views and give us support to maintain our chosen stance. In the process, there is the gratification of receiving approval, which offers all sorts of needed social reinforcement.

When it comes to selecting professional associates, attraction can be misleading. For example, perceived similarity may be based on a distortion, whereas actual similarity reveals qualities other than we have perceived. In the building of a relationship, such as an affiliation in a professional practice, perceived similarity is apt to be more important than actual similarity (Hill and Stull, 1981). Likewise, in the area of ability (such as clinical skills), people often develop misleading perceptions and ideas:

> People who are able, competent, and intelligent can provide many rewards. They can help us solve problems, give us advice, help us interpret world events, and so forth. It follows that competent, intelligent people are liked more than are incompetent, unintelligent people. Yet this proposition has

a major limitation. If a person is *too* perfect, we may feel uncomfortable or threatened. A too-perfect person also may be viewed as very dissimilar to ourselves in terms of attitudes, values, and so on, and this perceived dissimilarity also might decrease their attractiveness to us. Hence, persons who are extremely competent and intelligent might be liked more when they show a few human frailties than when they appear to be perfect [Brigham, 1986, pp. 194–195; emphasis in original].

We all want the best-trained and most clinically astute associates we can find, but it is possible that those assets, after affiliation, may become liabilities that result in an unsatisfactory business union.

In mental health, the common scenario has two practitioners with similar professional interests emphasizing a given procedure or treatment modality, preferring to work with a certain type of client, or relying on the same kinds of referral sources. The natural inclination is to think that this affiliation will be professionally stimulating. While this arrangement may be beneficial, it does have some drawbacks, such as giving the practice a rather narrow scope of services and placing the associates in (perhaps unwitting) competition with one another for referrals from the same sources.

Attraction and Complementarity. Complementarity is what Brigham (1986, pp. 541–542) defines as "the proposition that people with opposite personality characteristics may be attracted to each other." Research raises doubts about complementarity's ability to provide long-range satisfaction, at least in terms of personal and emotional liking (Brigham, 1986; Russ, Gold, and Stone, 1979, 1980).

In forming a practice group, the objective should be more than enjoying nice, warm feelings of liking. Successful task accomplishment is essential. If there are personal or emotional difficulties, the leader(s) of the group will be responsible for promoting resolution and reinstilling a positive atmosphere. The professional relationship thus goes beyond the dimension of liking, which is prevalent in friendship, and necessitates a blend of liking and competence. Since this blend is a prerequisite of effective professional relations, each practitioner should recognize that the affiliation is intended to do more than meet social and emotional needs.

Here, theories of complementarity become relevant. A professional relationship that hinges on varied objectives (rather than just on friendship) and includes interchanges concerned with specific issues or problems can satisfy needs and preferences through complementarity (Russ, Gold, and Stone, 1979, 1980). In a practice group, dissimilarity (such as among practitioners with different therapeutic stances) can still yield a healthy and productive group atmosphere. In part, one's professionalism embraces one's right to be different (if this is based on academically acceptable grounds) and one's right to "academic freedom." Professional complementarity can also generate financial rewards for all members of the practice group.

The effects of complementarity also depend on professional respect and acceptance, which engender reciprocal liking: The professional criteria cultivate a motivation to like one another for more than social and emotional reasons. If a practitioner perceives that a colleague responds to him or her with liking, he or she is apt to reciprocate (if, however, the other person's response is interpreted as ingratiation, there will be a negative reciprocal response—ulterior motives backfire).

Propinquity. Complementarity also benefits from propinquity, or nearness. Liking can be accurately predicted by knowing who a person is closest to, whether at work or at home. For familiarity to lead to increased liking, however, there must be the expectation of continued interaction (Tyler and Sears, 1977, explain how propinquity works in everyday life). If two professionals who have worked together for years—say, in a public mental health hospital—decide to form a practice together, the new arrangement may allow them greater control over propinquity than they had in the hospital, and it may reduce their desire or need to maintain closeness.

Self-Disclosure. Mental health professionals typically possess one quality that will be helpful in overcoming any negative effects of complementarity: They are believers in self-disclosure. Of course, even mental health professionals vary in the degree of self-disclosure that they are willing to allow and in what they consider self-disclosure to be. For the purposes of forming a practice group, self-disclosure (as it might occur in staff conferences about case management) can allow professionals insight into colleagues' dissimilarity to themselves.

Creating a Match. There is no formula that will guarantee a perfect matching of professional colleagues. Given social-psychological research and the realities of the mental health business world, two guidelines merit consideration (even though the composition of each practice group is unique).

First, personal and professional similarity can produce an initial liking that does not necessarily meet long-range business objectives. Two professionals who share advocacy of a given therapeutic approach or interest in a specific service area may find their affiliation personally satisfying and academically stimulating; what is more likely, however, is that their practice will be restricted in scope, and a scope of service that is restricted by anything other than the market will attract fewer potential clients. For example, the market may not be able to accommodate enough of a single service within one practice, and so the colleagues will perhaps unknowingly be in competition for the same market section.

Second, professional complementarity may produce initial problems that will require effort and resources to solve, but—if the practice survives the early uneasiness, distrust, and turmoil—complementarity can provide long-term momentum and power. The practice group with wide professional complementarity will probably enjoy an ever expanding market for services, and the group's survival will be aided by its own dynamics.

Structural Forms for a Practice

Mental health professionals who choose to affiliate usually know little or nothing about legal alternatives for structuring the group. Since fixed conditions implicitly and explicitly characterize various business entities, professionals must seek legal advice (and probably tax advice from an accountant, too). It is foolish to enter into practice with the notion of trying it for a while and seeing how it works ("After we start making big bucks, we can always talk to a lawyer and an accountant"). The professional cannot afford a wait-and-see attitude.

To move into practice without the benefit of an appropriate business entity is to jeopardize funds, both in the short run (by incurring debts) and in the long run (by unnecessary relinquishment of profits to others). It will also increase one's legal risks (through vicarious liability for the malpractice of an affiliated professional) and lose tax and investment benefits. In other words, adequate legal and accounting information will allow one to select the best business entity for one's investment, financial, and liability concerns. (Nevertheless, no business entity ever provides total protection from the risks of the business world.)

Legal details about the forms of business that might be suitable for a mental health practice are available in Woody, 1988b. Since each state has its own laws, it is best to seek counsel from an attorney qualified to practice in the jurisdiction where the group will practice, and the same is true for seeking tax advice from an accountant.

Sole Proprietorship. Being a sole proprietor has appeal. It allows a practitioner to enter practice with little or no legal formality. Keep in mind that each locale may have unique requirements for permits, registrations, and taxation. Therefore, even a sole proprietorship is not free from governmental regulation, and legal counsel will be necessary.

While being a sole proprietor affords independence, it does not offer an opportunity to interact with a colleague on the spur of the moment. Mental health practice, particularly if it provides therapy, can be lonely and emotionally draining. The practitioner's personal health demands relaxed and cordial encounters. From the standpoint of risk management, having a colleague who can serve as a sounding board for treatment ideas maximizes the possibility of adequate care and reduces the likelihood of a malpractice suit. Similarly, obtaining supervision of one's cases from a colleague is an excellent legal safeguard against complaints (Woody, 1988a).

In terms of scope of service, the sole practitioner is restricted to accepting only those referrals for which he or she has treatment competence. This may mean turning certain clients away and losing them from the practice (if there were a partner with a different area of competence, however, the colleague could see the client). (Incidentally, a practice could include several professionals and yet be a sole proprietorship in that it would be owned by a single professional.)

Financially, the sole proprietorship depends on one person's ability to fund the practice. Even if there are associates working for the sole proprietor and paying an overhead fee, the ultimate financial burden, the decision making, and the duty to fulfill obligations fall to the sole proprietor.

Partnership. Having more than one owner spreads the financial responsibility and opens up additional resources for (among other things) operating at a superior level and marketing the practice to its fullest potential. It is common for mental health professionals to want to form partnerships. By definition, a partnership suggests equality for management decisions, profits and debts, and other liabilities. While there are legal differences among various locales, a contract typically could specify unequal involvement (for example, a limited partner usually invests money but has no say in operations) or ways of handling certain areas of liability. Even so, a partnership has drawbacks. For one thing, there are currently few if any tax benefits for a partnership that are not also available to a sole proprietor (as an individual taxpayer).

Equality is not always a dimension of wise business decisions. It may promote teamwork, but problems can arise if one partner does more than another and yet is not adequately compensated for his or her disproportionate effort or production.

In a general partnership, all partners are bound by the obligations of the partnership. There are two major liability problems with a general partnership. First, there can be *joint and several* liability. This means that if the partnership has a legal judgment entered against it and one partner has too few assets to fulfill his or her 50 percent share of the judgment, the plaintiff (such as a creditor) can collect more than 50 percent from the partner who has the ampler assets.

Second, there is *vicarious* liability. This means that a malpractice action against one partner may well also name other partners as allegedly liable because of their duty to protect clients (such as through adequate supervision), regardless of who was the treating therapist. Some forms of business entities in some jurisdictions afford a bit of protection from vicarious liability. In general, however, the mental health professional is subject to liability for the act (by omission or commission) of *anyone* (including support staff members) with whom he or she is linked by implicit or explicit responsibility. In this era of frequent malpractice actions, liability for someone else's conduct is of critical importance. Professionals must be completely familiar with the history and characteristics of everyone with whom they consider affiliating.

If a partnership is formed, it is wise (but perhaps not legally required, depending on the state) to prepare a highly specific written agreement. It must accord with the laws of the jurisdiction and should control all matters. Olle and Macaulay (1986) suggest that the agreement cover, among other items, a right to indemnification from the partnership for personal liabilities relevant to the partnership's business, provisions for accounting and legal actions between the partners, and specifics about tangible and intangible assets or property. It is also good to deal with what would happen upon the death of the partner; for example, how would the deceased partner's rights be transferred to his or her estate?

There are pluses and minuses to a mental health partnership. The financial rewards may come primarily through being able to develop a practice with a more comprehensive scope than a sole proprietorship would allow, reducing overhead and operating expenses, and having shared responsibility for business planning, financial resources, and marketing. Other benefits are psychological and personal: "gaining social-professional stimulation, exchanging theoretical and technical ideas to enhance the quality of service, and acquiring a sense of permanency and security for one's mental health practice" (Woody, 1988b, p. 71). Of course, there are negatives, such as joint and several liability, vicarious liability, loss of autonomy, and division of gain (including the "blue sky" value that usually increases with the longevity of the business). These negatives, especially liability, lead many practitioners to shy away from any form of professional affiliation or collective.

Corporation

There are various configurations for corporations. The most relevant ones are the *corporation for profit* (sometimes referred to as the C-corporation, because it is governed by Subchapter C of the Internal Revenue Code) and the *professional corporation* (different states give it different names, such as professional association, professional corporation, or professional services corporation). There can be a *corporation not for profit* (also known as a nonprofit corporation), but unless the mental health practice is aligned with a charitable organization, this form would be of little use. In each instance, the corporation is a legal entity separate from the persons who own it.

Corporate Taxation. Corporate taxation is different from taxation of the individual taxpayer. There is commonly "double taxation" of corporate revenues, meaning that the corporation pays an income tax and the shareholders pay tax on dividends. Consequently, the small group, with a limited number of partners who are also the sole or majority employees and who will need all the net profit to live on, might resist the idea of a corporation at first, because of double taxation.

To accommodate this situation, the Congress enacted

Subchapter S of the Internal Revenue Code, which "avoid[s] double taxation on earnings distributed to shareholders in a manner similar to sole proprietorships and partnerships. Moreover, losses generated by the Subchapter S corporation [are] permitted to be deducted on the shareholders' return, which ability was denied shareholders of regular corporations under the general Subchapter C provisions" (August and Bennett, 1986, p. 157). In keeping with the ever changing nature of taxation, the Subchapter S Revision Act of 1982 made substantial revisions, presumably eliminating problems and embracing principles similar to those applied to partnerships: "As a result, the tax impact of business operations conducted at the corporate level is passed through directly to the shareholders and reported as separate items of income, deduction, credit and loss rather than as an aggregate item composed of dividend income or net operating loss" (August and Bennett, 1986, p. 158). Electing the Subchapter S form for a profitable corporation may lower the taxes levied on profits distributed to shareholders, and double taxation of profits can be avoided.

Like every other form of corporation, the Subchapter S form has its complexities, pros, and cons. For example, the election of the Subchapter S form imposes limitations on the percentage of gross receipts derived from passive investments, such as dividends, royalties, interest, and rents. Given the constant changes in tax law, the selection of any corporate form should be made only after consultation with an attorney and an accountant, and that choice should be reappraised for suitability, probably on at least an annual basis.

The Corporate Shield. Regardless of its form, a corporation establishes shareholders' rights and usually shields the personal assets of shareholders from liability for corporate debts. For example, if a lease on expensive office space were taken out in the name of the corporation, or if expensive furniture and equipment were purchased in the name of the corporation, an unprofitable situation that required the closing of the practice would presumably limit creditors to seizing only those assets held by the corporation: They could repossess the furniture and the equipment but could not attach the practitioner-shareholders' personal assets. Of course, landlords and creditors are not naïve about this shield, and they commonly try to get tenants and debtors to sign leases or purchase orders "personally and for the corporation." This practice may remove the corporate shield.

The corporate shield for personal assets usually can be penetrated in malpractice cases. There are some limitations, but a malpractice judgment, whatever may be the corporate form surrounding its occurrence, will attach personal assets. Like all the other legal issues discussed in this book, this one involves various state laws; an essential safeguard is counsel from an attorney who is familiar with the laws that pertain to the jurisdiction in which the practitioner works.

Principles of Corporate Law. The powers of a corporation are governed by state law, with unique requirements to clarify its purpose, structure, and operations. A board of directors (which, in some states, can be one person) has management authority. Using bylaws or resolutions, the officers elected by the board of directors have responsibility for day-to-day management.

A shareholder may or may not be involved as a director or an officer. This arrangement allows the corporation to garner financial underwriting (as might be necessary to accomplish, for example, an effective marketing program). Too many mental health professionals fail to consider the benefits that could come from having investors. Instead, they restrict their budget planning to their personal funds or to loans (often at high interest rates). By virtue of being needed in the first place, a loan is apt to overburden cash flow (which, in a newly established practice, is unpredictable). An alternative is to analyze the pluses and minuses of allowing others to invest in the practice, whether they are other practitioners or nonprofessionals who are interested in profiting from investments. (If this alternative is explored, consideration should be given to the propriety of a nonprofessional's being involved, and to what a legally and ethically acceptable form for the involvement would be; for example, it would probably be illegal to include an unlicensed person as a shareholder in a professional corporation.)

The Professional Corporation. From a survey of state statutes covering professional corporations, Overcast and Sales (1981, p. 755) report that the states "have in common the requirements that the professionals who are able to incorporate must practice their professions pursuant to a license or certificate from a state regulatory board or licensing body." States vary in what disciplines they allow to use professional corporations. Some states require that all professionals in the professional corporation be of exactly the same discipline (for example, a psychologist could not form a professional corporation with a social worker, but if both disciplines had licensure, each professional could create his or her own professional corporation). Other states allow an amalgamation of disciplines (in states with this sort of law, a psychologist and a social worker could form a single professional corporation).

In general, the taxation issues for a professional corporation are comparable to those for a corporation for profit. Among other things, the professional corporation may contribute or deduct funds for profit-sharing plans, retirement plans, health insurance, disability insurance, life insurance, death benefits, and educational benefits (McGrath, 1986).

Depending on state law, the professional corporation may afford a certain amount of protection from vicarious liability: "Liability may be limited to negligent or wrongful acts or misconduct of the employees committed during the course of professional services. If the employee has committed the negligent or wrongful act outside the scope of employment—that is, 'on a personal frolic'—the professional individually and the corporation may be protected" (Woody, 1988b, p. 77). Generally, for the professional corporation or its individual owner to be held liable for the acts of another, a duty must exist to supervise the person who has allegedly committed the act. The professional corporation does not provide immunity. A plaintiff's attorney can be quite skilled at using public policy and a hired expert to construct a "duty to supervise."

As always, anyone interested in creating a professional corporation must seek advice about and analysis of the legal, financial, taxation, management, and investment issues from an attorney and an accountant. Additional information about professional corporations is available in Overcast and Sales (1981), Sales (1983), and Woody (1988b).

Contractual Conditions

If a business entity is formed, there will probably be some sort of registration with the state. For a corporation, articles of incorporation cast the tenets and the structure, as required by law, and by-laws are developed later to deal with governance and management. Even with legal prescriptions and proscriptions, there are always a lot of unattended issues or matters that are unique to the professional associates (referred to legally as "the parties") involved in the practice. As many issues or matters as possible should be covered in a written document. Since it is a mutually agreed-on document, it will be subject to contract law. For the sake of prudence, all formal agreements—and probably informal agreements as well—should be ratified by the parties only after each has received independent legal counsel. While one attorney may provide overall business-related counsel for the practice, an attorney cannot allow a conflict of interest. If there is a possible clash of interests among the parties, it may be necessary—and it would certainly be prudent and wise—for each practitioner to seek advice from his or her own independent attorney. Each attorney would concentrate only on the implications for one individual.

Agreements should be tailored to the situation and the parties. Experience reveals six areas that deserve special attention: the fiduciary duty, the financial obligation, the rights and duties, the compensation or remuneration, noncompetition and protection of trade secrets, and indemnification.

The Fiduciary Duty. When mental health professionals affiliate for a practice, there is an implied *fiduciary duty.* Some state statutes, such as for corporations or partnerships, make it an explicit duty. According to Olle and Macaulay (1986, p. 67), "This duty includes the following 'sub-duties' to: (1) provide full disclosure of all information concerning the partnership; (2)

refrain from competing with the partnership or otherwise deriv-
ing personal gain at the expense of the partnership; and (3)
exercise reasonable care with respect to partnership affairs."
(Olle and Macaulay use the word *partnership*, but the principle
is applicable to all business entities.)

Mental health professionals are prone to rely too much
on what is observable, to take a colleague at face value. This is
risky business. The principle of full disclosure encompassed by
the fiduciary duty justifies each associate's having access to virtually every personal bit of information about all the others,
and everyone in the practice that is being formed should report
such information voluntarily. (Unfortunately, there is sometimes a "Psychogate" within a practice when an associate covers
up certain character flaws from his or her colleagues.)

Fulfillment of the fiduciary duty demands information
on morals and values, sexual preferences, family relations (stability of marriage, problems with children), maladaptive habits,
substance use (alcohol, tobacco, recreational or street drugs,
prescribed medications), financial status (past and present income, debts, spending priorities), and so on. Disclosure must be
awarded dignity, respect, and confidentiality.

Some personal material will probably be difficult to deal
with. Risk management (say, for vicarious liability) makes it imperative that vulnerabilities be known beforehand. At the risk
of making what sound like "true confessions," the would-be
associates should all acknowledge any foibles, characteristics, or
behaviors that could be viewed as shortcomings. These are the
factors that could be sources later for ethical, regulatory, or
legal complaints. The old adage "Forewarned is forearmed" can
be heeded in a constructive and proactive manner. If any disclosure is too unsettling to be accepted by everyone, then the pro-
posed affiliation with the person who has made it should be
circumvented before it produces damage.

The Financial Obligation. For whatever reason, people find it
very difficult to talk about money. One's past and current debts
and spending habits are relevant to everyone else involved in a
practice, however, and should be disclosed. Likewise, there

must be no waffling about how much money will be needed to conduct the practice correctly, where the money will come from, and when the money must be paid. From the outset, the prospective associates should clearly understand the financial obligation that they all will be expected to meet.

The project's financial needs must be rationally based. Mental health practitioners seem to underestimate how much money will be needed. They tend to assume a cash flow that may be too idealistic, at least in the early stages of the practice. Seeking advice from an accountant or someone with special knowledge about mental health practice in a particular community can let a ray of reality shine into deliberations and planning.

With the force of contract law, an agreement among professionals should specify financial obligations for the individual and for the practice. With advice from legal counsel, the agreement should also stipulate what penalties will result from any associate's failure to meet the financial obligation.

Rights and Duties. Regardless of business entity, there should be an agreement about what an associate has a right to expect or gain and what he or she has a duty to fulfill. Among other things, this could include a right to indemnification (which will be discussed shortly), provisions for accounting and legal actions between associates, the method for making decisions (on expenditures, the admission of a new associate, the expulsion or dismissal of a professional), and specifics about tangible and intangible assets or property (distribution and maintenance of records upon dissolution of the group or upon the death of an associate).

A source of trouble is how much time and energy will be devoted by supposedly equal associates, how this will be assessed, and the consequences of failure to fulfill the duty. Mental health professionals tend to think that the agreement on duties will cover, at most, what therapy, assessment, or consultation services will be provided, by whom, and to what type of clients (and, possibly, how referrals will be divided). Those areas can be covered, but the agreement should also include an array of nonprofessional issues. Among troubled practice groups, untold problems could have been prevented by such agreements. (One group got into a dispute over whether each practitioner should be responsible for cleaning his or her own office and taking a turn at cleaning the common areas, or whether the group should hire a cleaning service.)

Compensation or Remuneration. Contract rights depend on compensation. Good business requires that money be dealt with in a straightforward, unapologetic manner. Money can lead to misunderstandings, and reservations about the way a colleague is dealing with money can escalate into major problems.

It is wise to have a definite policy about how fees for service will be determined (Will every practitioner in the group charge the same? How will the amount be determined?), when and how a reevaluation of the fee schedule will be conducted, and how debts will be collected.

Psychologically, it is helpful to allow each person to have a significant voice in determining the fee. The final determination, of course, must represent the best interests of the collective enterprise. Granted, if the mental health CEO is a sole proprietor employing associates, his or her views should carry the most weight. Even so, group cohesion will be facilitated if everyone affected by the fee policy is at least consulted.

Legally, the compensation and remuneration system for affiliated professionals must detail any money-related matters and have safeguards against subterfuge, fraud, or dishonesty of any kind. The seeking of third-party reimbursements from clients' insurance carriers must also be carefully monitored. In any event, compensation and remuneration must be forthright and unambiguous. Even a scintilla of questionable intent or the mere appearance of impropriety, accidental or not, transmits a message of unprofessionalism and perhaps even of illegality.

Noncompetition and Protection of Trade Secrets. The earlier definition of the fiduciary relationship revealed the duty to work for the welfare of all associates, as though it were one's personal welfare. Closely akin to the fiduciary duty is the notion that the affiliation will not be a proving ground for ideas that can be used in a competitive manner later on. It is best to bring this issue under the egis of contract law. An agreement should be prepared that defines proscriptions against unfair competition, as well as what will be deemed fair competition. The agreement will help avoid unnecessary disputes about post-affiliation activities. If there should, however, be an event that seems to be a wrongful breach of the agreement, contract law will offer a legal recourse.

A noncompetition clause in an agreement can provide for protection for all persons involved. Each state may have unique legal principles, by statute or case rulings, for defining an acceptable noncompetition agreement. A good example is Public Act Number 243, enacted by the Michigan Legislature in 1987, which states, in part:

> An employer may obtain from an employee an agreement or covenant which protects an employer's reasonable competitive business interests and expressly prohibits an employee from engaging in employment or a line of business after termination of employment if the agreement or covenant is reasonable as to its duration, geographical area, and the type of employment or line of business. To the extent any such agreement or covenant is found to be unreasonable in any respect, a court may limit the agreement to render it reasonable in light of the circumstances in which it was made and specifically enforce the agreement as limited.

This Michigan statute includes the essentials of the common or case law in most states—namely, that a noncompetition agreement is possible, but it must be reasonable in its terms. Reasonableness is often measured according to the length of time that the agreement restricts competition, the geographical area that is protected, and the type of business that is being foreclosed. In some jurisdictions, strict scrutiny is applied to noncompetition covenants, especially when professional services may be restricted that would otherwise benefit the public.

When these principles are applied to a mental health practice, there is no specific limit for time, geography, or service. With deference to the laws of the particular jurisdiction, the following general guidelines are offered.

1. Clinical practice might be subject to noncompetition for, say, two to five years, with the longer period being available to a practice that provides a specialized service, has self-created methods and systems, and relies on definite referral sources or client pools.
2. The reasonable geographical boundary might be influenced by the nature of the service, referral sources, and clients (such as where previous clients came from within the designated area and what the total population or client pool was for the designated area).
3. The more general the practice and the less specialized its methods, systems, referral sources, and client pool, the more limited would be the protection from competition. Whatever the wording of the contract, the interpretation would give some weight to the intent of the parties, fairness and equity, and any special considerations, such as impact on third parties (for example, the community's need for mental health services).

Affiliated professionals in a group practice certainly should address the noncompetition issue before initiating their service. Associates' leaving group practices and "stealing clients" or "interfering with referral sources" has been a major source of ill will and legal complaints. Usually no one survives this sort of dispute without permanent scarring. For example, attempts to take one's records when one leaves have met with lawsuits to declare the records the property of the practice, and they usually are (unless this point is specified otherwise by agreement, the original group usually has a limited property right to the records, although the departing professional may be entitled to a photocopy).

Particularly troubling is the "ownership" of clients. Obviously, no professional owns a client. Even when there is an agreement that prohibits a departing professional from soliciting former clients who were served through the practice group, clients are free to seek service elsewhere. If the "elsewhere" happens to be in the departed practice member's office, little can be done—unless there was, for example, an agreement calling for payment of, say, a percentage over a specific and reasonable time, of all funds collected from clients the practitioner originally saw in the practice group. Such an obligation could be based on the original group's interest in the case, the group having made payments for advertising to attract the client and bring the business to the practitioner, and on its continuing liability for the welfare of the client.

Wrongful competition has often been alleged by supervisors (in clinical practice) against former trainees. The trainee, hungry for an enriching supervised experience, enters a clinical practice. Upon completion of the internship or field experience, the trainee-graduate may sense an obligation to continue to see a client or may wish to set up a practice that draws from the clientele seen during training. If there is no objection from the supervisor or no contract to the contrary, such an arrangement is acceptable.

Sometimes the trainee has agreed to be noncompetitive. The trainee has been informed ahead of time of policies against competition; he or she thereby implicitly endorses the policy. Perhaps the trainee has signed a contract explicitly precluding competition within a reasonable framework. Upon completion of training, the trainee-graduate is chagrined to be reminded of the noncompetition contract. Detrimental emotions, "bad mouthing," and other negative conditions ensue, and everyone loses, supervisor and trainee alike.

When arranging field experiences, university faculty members have a duty to help field supervisors and trainees clarify all critical conditions, including (but certainly not limited to) the liability that probably attaches to a supervisor-trainee relationship and to potential problems, like posttraining competition. A supervisor-practitioner would be foolish to accept a trainee without careful risk-management arrangements, including a noncompetition agreement.

If there is a violation of a noncompetition agreement, the legal process is open to the aggrieved. Causes of actions are varied, but they may include breach of contract and tortious interference with a business contract.

Finally, there are some aspects of a clinical practice that merit protection as trade secrets. Clients' names, mailing lists, forms used for internal record keeping, computer programs, assessment methods, clients' "homework" assignments, and numerous other management and service aids may be protected from use by others. Unless protection is specified by statute (for example, copyright) and/or by contract, the protection upheld by a court of law will probably depend on the circumstances.

The primary point is that being an insider, whether a professional peer or a trainee in the practice group for a limited time, affords insights into what makes a mental health practice a success or a failure. The ethics and laws for business recognize this as a situation that must not be exploited and that must therefore be subject to legal recourse.

Perhaps the epitome of support from public policy for noncompetition obtains when the owner of a practice "sells" it to another practitioner. Implied in the sale is that the practice has some "blue sky" value—that is, it is an operating and established business with some worth (more than would be vested with a new business), and this worth is greater than the "hard" assets. Therefore, it is common for the buy-sell agreement to include a reasonably framed covenant not to compete—that is, the seller will not open a competing business or work for a competitor of the practice being sold. While public policy and its laws support fair competition, for the sake of consumers' welfare, insider status could be an avenue to obtain an edge on the competition and thus be unfair and detrimental to society. Covenants that preclude professional services that could benefit the public often get strict scrutiny. While a noncompetition covenant applied to a professional may be upheld by a court of law, the noncompetition would have to be amply justified (in contrast to, say, noncompetition in a nonessential service).

To ensure protection of trade secrets, the associates should have an agreement that specifies what happens upon the departure of a professional or a layperson. Any person allowed entry into the practice should be prepared to pledge that he or she will safeguard information about how the practice is conducted or operated. There must be no revelations of the unique management or operational strategies, procedures, materials, and so on, to any outside (competitive) source. In keeping with the fiduciary duty, the agreement should make it clear that the person must not use insider knowledge for his or her personal gain at the expense of the former associates (for example, by providing a subsequent employer with information about how the previous employer's practice achieved success or failure).

This justifiable need to protect has led to abrupt and unamicable terminations of associates and employees. Although they sometimes seem justified by the circumstances and personalities involved, heavy-handed terminations can produce long-lasting bad feelings that will lead to hostile interprofessional relations in later years. A hostile parting of the ways may also produce a lawsuit to determine whether the employer's action was appropriate. Moreover, abrupt terminations disregard the best interests of the clients being treated by the departed associate. If the clients are to continue receiving good care from the same mental health facility, the established therapist should be allowed to implement therapeutic termination with each client and to facilitate a transition, if necessary, to another therapist on the staff (perhaps the two therapists can hold a joint session with the client to implant their shared responsibility and caring).

Few mental health professionals are willing or able to think about the termination of an association when they are struggling with the formation of a practice. Being proactive on these matters, however, can provide much-needed definition for the business operations from the outset and avoid the possibility of future professional conflicts, legal expenses, and risks with clients.

Indemnification. The fiduciary duty spans ethics and the law and can impose sanctions for any breach. Again, a proactive alternative, such as a clear-cut agreement, eliminates any misconceptions, provides guidance for conduct, and sets the damages that may ensue from a breach of duty. Indemnification is an important contractual tool for constructing the fiduciary duty.

Indemnification means, simply, that a person who incurs expense due to another person's omissions or commissions is entitled to compensation. As Olle and Macaulay (1986, pp. 67–68) explain it, "Partners have a right to indemnification from the partnership for personal liabilities incurred or payments made on behalf of the partnership in the course of the partnership's business. In addition, when one partner is required to contribute more than his pro rata share to satisfy a liability or obligation of the partnership, he has an action against the other partners on a pro rata basis for the excess." In accord with risk management, a professional can require an indemnification contract from another professional or from a health-care facility. For example, if the professional is sued on the basis of his or her vicarious liability for the alleged malpractice of an associate, a previously established indemnification agreement could prescribe that the alleged malfeasor would pay the first professional's legal expenses.

Although this is only an example of an agreement (and is not suitable for adoption in any specific instance, without legal counsel), Woody (1988b, p. 53) offers the following indemnification statement: "The employer agrees to indemnify the mental health professional for any threatened, pending, or completed claim, whether civil, criminal, administrative, or investigative, by reason of the fact of the commission or omission, professionally, by the employer or one of its other employees, with said indemnification being for all expenses (including fees), judgments, fines, and amounts paid in settlement."

Some mental health professionals choose to ignore warnings about the elevated risk in certain roles, such as when one provides diagnostic services in a high-risk medical area (for example, to a pain clinic or a neurology group). They reason that if they set too many conditions, such as an indemnification arrangement, they will lose potential income. That may be true, but in this litigious age, the prudent mental health practitioner cannot afford to lose sight of his or her goal to come out ahead in the long run. Several good years of income from, say, an independent contract with a high-risk medical practice can be wiped out if one is named in a lawsuit that is based on vicarious liability for medical malpractice. An indemnification agreement places responsibility for damages on the source of the cause for legal action.

In a mental health group, indemnification can be a means of risk management. The most trusting and dedicated partners should want to maintain responsibility for themselves and not impose the effects of any personal shortcomings on their colleagues in the practice. Indemnification focuses everyone's attention on maintaining a respectable and legally safe standard of care. Woody (1988b) provides more details about indemnification.

Advantages and Disadvantages of a Group Practice

The preceding material has revealed numerous benefits and liabilities of an affiliation between professionals. (Chapter Six will explore group dynamics in the context of a mental health practice, with emphasis on selecting and supervising professional associates and support staff members alike.)

The mental health practitioner must carefully assess the possibility of affiliating with other professionals and, if this is accepted, structure the group situation in a manner that will afford legal protection, maximize benefits and minimize liabilities, and accommodate monitoring and alterations as the group moves ahead in the health-care business.

The decision of whether to be an independent practitioner or to be affiliated with other professionals in a group practice may well be the most critical determinant of business success. This decision provides an occasion for the practitioner to get necessary help and prevent problems.

Perhaps the reasons that initially lead a person to be a professional caregiver also contribute to the tendency or need to affiliate with a practice group. There appears to be an increase in the proportion of group practices to solo practices, which may be a product, in part, of this new business era for mental health practice. Mental health practice today is more impersonal and business-oriented than it used to be, and joining a group practice may afford social and personal reinforcement. Part of the attraction of a practice group is surely the fulfillment of the personal needs unique to caregivers. By having others around, the practitioner can use colleagues to counteract the loneliness of the therapy room.

A group practice can also produce marketing and operational benefits. If two affiliated practitioners are not competing for the same clients (that is, if they have professional complementarity), the funds spent to promote one practitioner are potentially doubled in value because they also promote the other (for example, through an advertisement in the yellow pages). In the financial realm, certain operational or overhead expenses can be reduced substantially if the members of a practice group share costs. Revenue can be increased through cross-referrals. Among themselves, colleagues can refer clients for special services, thereby enhancing the quality of care and keeping clients' fees within the practice group.

Risk management involves different considerations, however. On the one hand, risk can be lessened if others are readily available for supervision, consultation, and special services to upgrade the standard of care. On the other hand, vicarious liability can have awesome implications. It is never possible to have total assurance that there will be no risk from associating with others; a major safeguard can be obtained only through investing resources in mutual supervision. Not the least expenditure will be time, with each group member needing to allocate time to stay familiar with what his or her colleagues are doing, monitor the quality of their work, and take steps to rectify any shortcomings. In other words, a group practice imposes both risks and a financial burden.

CHAPTER 6

Managing Group Dynamics: Selecting and Supervising Associates and Staff

THE MENTAL HEALTH CEO IS RESPONSIBLE FOR EF-fective management of human resources. Human resources include laypersons and professionals associated with the practice. Resource management is predicated on maximizing the contributions of the associates, with consideration being given to environmental factors, organizational system(s), role definitions, and individual characteristics (Hall and Goodale, 1986). This chapter emphasizes the organizational premise of the practice as a group, ways for individual characteristics to be dealt with for business effectiveness, and supervisory strategies available to the mental health CEO—all with the goal of maximizing entrepreneurship.

The Mental Health Practice as a Group

Group dynamics has long been a mainline topic in the behavioral sciences. From industrial and military management, a multitude of research studies have documented that when people come together, the outcome is more than what each individual contributes: The whole is greater than the sum of the parts. This premise is applicable to the mental health practice group.

Entrepreneurship calls for efforts that will capitalize on

any available resource, and group dynamics constitutes a critical resource. The associates in the mental health practice group are not merely an aggregate of professionals—that is, a class or collection of people who happen to be in the same place, each doing his or her own "thing"; rather, the practice group is interactive. Moreover, "the group . . . is not only interactive, it is also *dynamic*. It is a group whose members are in a continuously *changing* and *adjusting* relationship with reference to one another" (Bonner, 1959, p. 4; emphasis in original). In other words, the formation of the group engenders a quest whose goals are uniquely different from those of individual quests, and a dynamic interaction produces all sorts of effects.

Change is an integral part of a group: "Individuals form a group if they believe a specific situation should be changed and that one person acting alone cannot create the change" (Zander, 1985, p. 1). Professionalism certainly increases the change dimension in a group. The desire to be a better professional motivates the practitioner to accept new information and make service adaptations. Unfortunately, professionalism is not always sufficient to guarantee that the practitioner will change for the better. Like everyone else, a mental health professional may be prone, because of personal characteristics, to resist altering the attitudes, skills, and procedures acquired during an earlier stage of career development. Making rational changes, such as adopting risk-management strategies, is a prerequisite of entrepreneurship.

Virtually all interacting persons experience a state of tension (being attracted or repelled) and seek to resolve it or to restore equilibrium among themselves (the concept of homeostasis). Departing and arriving members foster a press for change in the nature and operations of the group. Change in the group structure and functions may be resisted, and the CEO must bring about constructive flexibility. As Bonner (1959, pp. 5–6) summarizes, "A dynamic group is thus in a continuous process of restructuring, adjusting, and readjusting members to one another for the purpose of reducing the tensions, eliminating the conflicts, and solving the problems which its members have in common."

Through its roots in academic reasoning and logic, professionalism has the potential of increasing flexibility and constructive change. Conversely, professionalism can also be a source of dogmatic adherence to the traditional, firmly ingrained ideas of the past. Faced with the rapid induction of mental health practice into the world of business, mental health professionals sometimes experience an unjustified defensiveness toward change. For example, even though a professional code of ethics has been modified to accommodate a public policy change (say, about advertising), some practitioners cling to outdated and inapplicable ethical notions.

The Healthy Practice Group. A mental health practice group should constantly seek to be a healthy organization. According to Bion (1961, pp. 25-26), "good group spirit" is demonstrated by the following characteristics:

(a) A common purpose, whether that be overcoming an enemy or defending and fostering an ideal or a creative construction in the field of social relationships or in physical amenities.

(b) Common recognition by members of the group of the "boundaries" of the group and their position and function in relation to those of larger units or groups.

(c) The capacity to absorb new members, and to lose members without fear of losing group individuality—i.e., "group character" must be flexible.

(d) Freedom from internal sub-groups having rigid (i.e., exclusive) boundaries. If a sub-group is present it must not be centred on any of its members nor on itself—treating other members of the main group as if they did not belong within the main group barrier—and the value of the sub-group to the function of the main group must be generally recognized.

(e) Each individual member is valued for his contribution to the group and has free movement within it, his freedom of locomotion being limited only by the generally accepted conditions devised and imposed by the group.

(f) The group must have the capacity to face discontent within the group and must have means to cope with discontent.

(g) The minimum size of the group is three. Two members have personal relationships; with three or more there is a change of quality (interpersonal relationship).

Applying these criteria to a mental health practice, we can see that the associates have the common purpose of building and maintaining a professional practice that will yield maximum benefits (personal, financial, or whatever). The common purpose will mean entering into the competitive marketplace composed of other mental health practitioners and being united and reciprocally supportive in the business endeavor. The mental health practice group must have clear definitions that include each member's intra- and intergroup allegiances. As necessary and justifiable, new professionals should be brought into the group; and, regardless of the length of their affiliation or friendships within the group, members who do not contribute adequately to the group objectives must be allowed to leave. Within the group, each professional should have the opportunity to develop personally and professionally, relying on his or her group identity and the group's resources to meet individual needs and goals. Discontent within or cleavage from the group should be confronted and resolved, with avoidance of personal animosity or denigration. Personal relationships among associates can and will exist, but membership in the group requires supreme dedication.

Reasons for Joining a Mental Health Practice Group. There are personal and professional reasons that lead mental health practitioners to join together in a practice group. Worchel and Cooper (1983) point out that, on the personal level, humans have a need to belong and affiliate, groups can be a source of important information that will assist people with crucial aspects of life, groups give rewards, groups facilitate goal achievement that would otherwise be beyond one individual's grasp, and self-identity is gained from group membership.

In the mental health practice group, the professional can find much-needed emotional support and fulfill his or her need to be accepted by others. For the professional, a sense of belonging to a practice with high-status colleagues makes the affiliation especially powerful for need fulfillment. It attests to the practitioner's competence and career success. Such social recognition may be prized more highly than a monetary reward. Providing mental health services can also be exhausting. Being a therapist is emotionally draining, and even a brief respite over a cup of coffee with a colleague may buttress the therapist for subsequent involvement with clients. Interaction with other professionals yields valuable information about how to improve the quality of care. Risk management is enhanced by colleagues' information, supervision, and ideas about how to manage or help troublesome clients. The rewards of a group practice can be as concrete as reduced overhead expenses through the sharing of costs, or increased income through a complementary referral system among associates. A comprehensive mental health services group allows each practitioner to benefit from the association: experiencing stimulating teamwork (through interactions with professionals who have diverse skills and interests), gaining safeguards against malpractice, and receiving the opportunity for specialized referrals.

The Unhealthy Practice Group. Unfortunately, there are many mental health practice groups that fail to achieve a healthy status. Indeed, there may be clear organizational pathology; the old adage "Physician, heal thyself" comes readily to mind.

If the entrepreneurial effort is not handled adroitly, the mental health CEO, like anyone else subjected to intense emotional pressure and conflict, can become dysfunctional. In management operations, this dysfunction could be manifested as a character disorder or neurotic personality pattern.

Similarly, the personalities of the associated professionals and the support staff members can combine to produce a dysfunctional group. At either the individual or the group level, the result will probably be faulty planning and implementation, weakening of the organizational structure and culture, and inept decision making.

The overall mental health services organization can also become ill. One of the most harmful conditions that can exist in any kind of organization is "groupthink." Janis (1983, p. 9) describes this condition as follows: "I use the term . . . as a quick and easy way to refer to a mode of thinking that people engage in when they are deeply involved in a cohesive in-group, when the members' strivings for unanimity override their motivation to realistically appraise alternative courses of action . . . . Groupthink refers to a deterioration of mental efficiency, reality testing, and moral judgment that results from in-group pressures." According to Worchel and Cooper (1983, pp. 509–510), "Groupthink results because the group members become so concerned over keeping a high degree of consensus and cohesiveness that they suspend their reality-testing powers and fail to exercise their ability to critically evaluate ideas." Given the intimate nature of the services in this kind of relatively closed system (able to exclude, although unwisely, external inputs and controls), it may well be that the mental health practice group may be more vulnerable to groupthink than other types of organizations are.

Groupthink can lead the practice group to be shortsighted and closed-minded. Worchel and Cooper (1983) suggest that groupthink produces six symptoms. First, there is a group-held illusion of invulnerability: "No other mental health practice group provides as high a quality of service as we do!" Second, the group members consider themselves to possess a high degree of morality: "We always operate ethically and put the welfare of clients ahead of making huge profits, which is more than you can say for our competitors." Third, there are commonly held intragroup stereotypes about persons and issues outside the practice group: "We all know about those charlatans at the XYZ Clinic; they shouldn't be allowed to practice." Fourth, there is an illusion of agreement and unanimity, even when diversity of opinion exists: "Well, we've heard some differing views today, but we can chalk those up to our various theoretical bents—we all know than none of us would rock the boat, and we are in agreement about how to proceed." Fifth, there are strong pressures for all group practice members to conform, and each member, even though he or she is a professional, becomes reluctant to express disagreement; this is true even when he or she holds a more reasonable view: "It's very important that we stick together on this matter. If it gets outside this room that we differ, we could lose the client or even be sued for malpractice." Sixth, a strong, forceful, and respected leader reinforces the thrust toward agreement and docility: "Being the CEO for our group, I know that our shared mission will keep us united, shoulder to shoulder, and none of us will risk making matters worse by arguing or fighting among ourselves."

Groupthink can be counteracted. Woody (1987, p. 575) discusses the symptoms of groupthink and notes that treatment may have to come from outside the practice group: "Outside professional help may be needed, namely a consultant who can: (1) analyze objectively the functioning . . . ; (2) offer specialized behavioral-science information that can enhance the deliberations and interactions; and (3) facilitate effective communication—all to improve the quality of the decision-making processes." This recommendation stems from two facts: first, groupthink is seldom recognized by the impeded organization; and, second, practitioners are often reluctant to invest in professional management resources (such as hiring a consultant) and prefer the risk of continuing mediocre and/or detrimental decision making.

Sometimes group pathology is less obvious. Instead of on a global effect, the focus can be on a two-person relationship. Of course, even a dyadic infection can fester into a full-blown organizational lesion. This organizational health risk can best be diagnosed through ever vigilant supervision by and leadership from the mental health CEO.

Moving to a more microcosmic level, an individual can be a carrier of a germ of organizational pathology. Everyone has his or her ups and downs, such as a divorce or a period of existential uncertainty, and the mental health practice group is not immune to injury from a single member. Tolerance, support, and humane considerations should certainly be extended to the troubled member of the practice group, and encouragement should be given to his or her finding treatment.

It is interesting that mental health practitioners who have, for example, violated propriety in the therapist-client relationship (for example, through sexual misconduct) will seldom acknowledge that the proscribed behavior was due to a character flaw. Similarly, when there is a problem member, it is common for his or her colleagues, although they are highly trained in mental health services, to ignore, deny, or fail to recognize the presence of a significant character or personality problem.

Needless to say, the "buck stops" with the mental health CEO, who must take decisive action with the troubled or dysfunctional member for the welfare of the organization. Summarizing their research on the "neurotic organization," Kets de Vries and Miller (1984, pp. 207–208) warn: "Neurotic styles, groups sharing basic assumptions, transference patterns, resistances, superior/subordinate entanglements, and position in the career life cycle can all have a dramatic impact on organizational performance . . . these forces can lead to impulsive decision making, severe morale problems, inadequate leadership, and untenable strategies and structures. Organizational consultants simply cannot afford to ignore these factors as contributors to the problems that they so often find themselves struggling with." In this instance, the term *consultant* should not obscure that the same responsibility rests on the shoulders of the CEO. The mental health CEO should welcome any possible source for remediating pathological conditions within the organization. This may require an outside professional to push for the understanding and change that will be necessary. Kets de Vries and Miller (1984, p. 208) assert: "Sometimes the only way to change the organization's behavior is to change the behavior of its principal actors. And the only way to do that is to convince them *that* they are wrong, to show them *why* they are wrong, and to give them at least some insight into the genesis of their dysfunctional attitudes, beliefs, and actions" (emphasis in original).

Insight must reach to organizational problems and the people who work, manage, and control the mental health practice group. This will require open-mindedness, time, and resources: "Much time and effort are required to make these discoveries, and the process of diagnosis can be disquieting for both the executives and the consultant" (Kets de Vries and Miller, 1984, p. 208). Again, it should be remembered that being an expert in human behavior can be a double-edged sword for the mental health practitioner. While it can facilitate cognitive understanding, it may construct emotional barriers, with such defense mechanisms as the attitude "What can a consultant tell me that I don't already know?"

The Supremacy Rule

Entrepreneurship embraces the *Supremacy Rule:* A member of a business group must be dedicated to the welfare of the organization above his or her own welfare. This vestige of institutionalization can be very troubling to the mental health professional who holds collegial relations sacrosanct.

In practical terms, the Supremacy Rule means that each member of the group must always make a necessary and adequate contribution to the group; there is no preordained right to remain now and forever in the practice group. Admission and retention are objectively determined by criteria and assessment methods accepted by the group.

Most often, professional groups base their admission decisions on the candidate's established credentials (such as a degree from a reputable university and licensure) and potential to be successful in practice (based on his or her ability to communicate effectively and propose ideas for marketing the practice, as determined by interviews). Professional groups base their retention decisions on the associate's ability to be a "rainmaker," (bringing in new business, generating profits, and surpassing his or her own share of the overhead) and his or her enhancement of the group's professional image (including through social and community roles and leadership in professional circles). In the business enterprise, there is no room for sentimentality or undying friendship; personal relationships must be separated from business efforts. If personal and business relationships can coexist, fine. If there is ever a lessening of someone's contribution to the business goals, however, it cannot be mitigated by friendship alone.

There may be a time when, out of personal allegiance, the group will be magnanimous to a member who is no longer pulling his or her share of the business load. Perhaps the member has devoted years to building the practice (with much of that effort having been uncompensated at the time) and finds that he or she can no longer stay abreast of the academic or practice demands that the contemporary scene requires. Or perhaps a member's ill health deserves special consideration (such as compensation beyond an income-protection insurance policy). Reduced or quasi-retirement assignments can be arranged that will allow ongoing compensation to the less productive member, and the group will feel satisfied (and thus motivated to produce) by having taken care of one of its own at a time of transition or crisis.

As unpleasant as it may be, the mental health CEO bears the responsibility of governing the admission and retention systems within the practice group. Ideally, there will be policies and procedures that are known and influenced by all concerned. In the long run, it remains for the CEO to implement whatever procedure is necessary to accomplish the change necessary to protect the practice group's quest. The policies should include options for, say, a senior partner who, notwithstanding a peerless contribution to the group in the past, should now relinquish his or her role for the benefit of the group. If policies are developed before an actual problem arises, they are most likely to be accepted by all and to honor the welfare of both the individual member and the practice group.

Developing a Group Purpose

In the context of managing human resources, the reason that brings mental health practitioners together must be constantly evaluated and maintained, to maximize the group members' functioning and their movement toward business goals. The characteristics, competence, and qualities (positive and negative) of the members will flesh out any structure that has been built through legal consultation and business planning. Consequently, great emphasis should be placed on selecting and retaining only those people who will make a continuing contribution to the organization. The first step in this area of human resources management is having a group purpose.

As mentioned earlier, individuals form a group partly because of a belief that there is a specific situation that should be changed, as well as a sense that the group will be able to accomplish the task better than an individual could. The specific situation that is the subject of change constitutes the framework for the purpose of the group: "The purpose provides a direction for activities, and members are uncomfortable if they do not have this guide. It tells members what they ought to do and what they can expect of colleagues. It offers a criterion for evaluating whether the efforts of the members are as effective as they ought to be. It is a focus for the personal commitment a member might make to that unit. It may serve, after the fact, as a rationalization for actions members take before they have a precise aim for their efforts. It reduces participants' sense of aimlessness in their work for that unit" (Zander, 1985, p. 92). (A glance back at the earlier section on reasons for joining a mental health group will reveal numerous possible purposes.)

Once the associates have come together to form a practice group (whatever its legal structure), the fundamental purpose should be set forth. Zander (1985) believes that the developers must declare the purpose, and the group's purpose should serve as an incentive to keep the members in and working for the group. If a difference in purpose develops, the CEO (and other members as well) will try to reduce the differences and develop a common point of view. Zander (p. 7) points out that it is unlikely that the purpose will remain fixed: "The quality of the problem-solving procedures used by those who organize or join a group may modify the content of the purposes defined for the body." Likewise, the values of the decision makers and the motives of all members will limit their freedom of choice in selecting or endorsing a purpose. The members must sense that the purpose of the group will allow them adequate satisfaction. Consequently, they are attracted to clear (measurable and accessible) objectives, and they like appropriate activities.

Several of the preceding comments underscore how important it is that the group's purpose meet the needs of the members. Members may have idiosyncratic individual motives for teaming up with others to act on a shared motive. Zander (1985, p. 127) clarifies:

> A motive is a capacity to find satisfaction in the attainment of a given incentive and a disposition to seek that satisfaction. A member may have a self-oriented motive or a group-oriented motive (called a desire for the group). A group purpose or goal is an incentive. The strength of a motive is indicated by the tendency of a member to behave in accord with it. The strength of a tendency is determined by the capacity to be satisfied by a given state of affairs (motive), the existence of a state that, if attained, will provide more or less satisfaction (incentive), and an estimate of the chances that the satisfaction can be reached (perceived probability). The stronger the incentive, the perceived probability, and the motive, the more a person will be active in accord with the motive. This is true regardless of whether the motive is for self alone or for the entire group.

Too often, mental health practitioners come together with no more than a nominal consideration of why they are affiliating ("We can cut down on expenses if we share office space"). This sort of reason is actually no reason—at least, no logical business reason, and certainly no entrepreneurial reason. True, individual needs are to be fulfilled, but the practice group should concentrate its hiring and retention functions on people who can contribute significantly to the group purpose.

Entrepreneurship requires all members of the group, led

by the CEO, to enter into considered analysis and deliberations of the professional and business purposes of the practice group, and the conclusions must allow for effective business planning. Without a statement of purpose, the practice group will, at best, aimlessly meander along a quasi-business route. With a definitive purpose, the practice group will be able to select and retain the best troops to march forth along a road to business victory.

Selecting and Supervising Support Staff Members

Selecting support staff members (such as secretaries) is important for the efficacious achievement of business goals and for risk management. Professional and support staff members should be accepted into the practice group solely for their ability to contribute constructively and significantly to the mission and to the short- and long-term objectives.

While family allegiance may lead to a professional's bringing a spouse or offspring into the office to work, it should be recognized that this can create problems. First, if the choice of a family member has been for reasons other than competence, a business objective may suffer. Second, the mixing of roles can lead to conflict. For example, one senior practitioner, who was considering recommendations for a more efficient management system, concluded, "The ideas are excellent and certainly would lead to an improvement over what happens now, but my wife serves as office manager and many of these changes will lead her to refuse to cooperate—I have a difficult time convincing her that when I want something done in the office, it is a professional decision and not her husband's opinion."

There may be tax benefits from hiring a family member. One practitioner paid his daughter about three times more than he would have paid someone else, reasoning that this kept the money in the family and allowed his daughter to pay a lower tax than he would have paid on the same money. This may be an acceptable arrangement, but caution should be exercised to avoid some type of family payment arrangement that violates tax laws or the rules of the Internal Revenue Service.

Problems can also arise from hiring a client. Presumably

for altruistic motives, the mental health practitioner may feel sorry for a client who needs income and hire him or her to do, say, secretarial work. At first glance, this move may appear to be helpful. On closer scrutiny, a red flag goes up over the possible ulterior (perhaps unconscious) motive behind the practitioner's controlling attempt to shift a client out of a helpee role and into a colleague/employee role. The ethical principle relevant to inappropriate dual relationships, common to virtually all human services disciplines, may be violated. Moreover, the practitioner's potential to provide further treatment to the client may be diluted, diminished, impeded, or eliminated. One practitioner hired a client to work as a secretary in the office, to "help her pay for her therapy." After a short time, it became evident that she lacked the skills to do the job adequately. The practitioner was faced with the dilemma of firing her—certainly a negative evaluative communication—while wanting to continue to be her therapist. As might be expected, her termination ended up being in both the employment and therapeutic realms. This sort of scenario gives rise to speculation about whether the motives of the practitioner are in the best interests of the client (as ethics and law require) or are self-serving: There was an opportunity to obtain cheap labor (the client's salary was low) or there may have been greed (the client was able to keep paying for treatment). There may also have been unresolved countertransference.

Hiring anyone for reasons that do not advance business goals and enhance risk management is contrary to the principles of entrepreneurship. Beyond being a poor business practice, it can harbor a wrongful professional purpose. Nominal involvement of ambiguously qualified family members may sometimes advance business and professional purposes; hiring clients never does. The only entrepreneurial justification for hiring anyone else is competence.

Risk management also depends on selecting and retaining for competence. Fulfilling a reasonable standard of care is an ever present mandate in mental health practice. While this mandate is normally thought of in terms of a professional's providing an acceptable quality of service to avoid an allegation of malpractice, the principle is also applicable to support staff members. The highly sensitive nature of mental health services, including clients' right to confidentiality and privileged communication, places an obligation on professionals and support staff members alike to further clients' best interests. Faulty judgment on the part of a support staff member can injure a client. For example, if a secretary wrongfully releases confidential records to, say, the employer of a client, and the employer decides, because of the information, that the client is "too crazy" to continue being employed, a legal action may allege liability both for the support staff member and for the professional.

It is imperative that every employee be properly trained. The prudent mental health CEO will not assume anything about competence. No matter what a new employee's past work experience has been, orientation, training, and ongoing supervision are necessary to ensure, as much as possible, that there will be no faulty judgments or avoidable errors on the part of the employee. This type of human resources management requires time (for supervision) and money (aside from the time expenditure, perhaps the cost of a seminar on risk management). Like many other expenditures, these expenses (including the allocation of supervisory time) should be viewed as a reasonable necessity of doing business in today's mental health market and as an investment in organizational development.

An employer (a "master") is legally responsible for the acts, omissions, or commissions of his or her employee (the "servant"):

> A multitude of very ingenious reasons have been offered for the vicarious liability of a master: he has a more or less fictitious "control" over the behavior of the servant; he has "set the whole thing in motion," and is therefore responsible for what has happened; he has selected the servant and trusted him, and so should suffer for his wrongs, rather than an innocent stranger who has had no opportunity to protect himself; it is a great concession that any man should be permitted to employ

another at all, and there should be a corresponding responsibility as the price to be paid for it—or, more frankly and cynically, "In hard fact, the reason for the employers' liability is the damages are taken from a deep pocket" [Keeton, Dobbs, Keeton, and Owen, 1984, p. 500].

Perhaps above all else, there is the premise that a person who stands to benefit financially from a business enterprise must protect the consumers. The potential for financial payoff leads to a purposeful allocation of risk. As Keeton, Dobbs, Keeton, and Owen (1984, pp. 500–501) describe it:

> The losses caused by the torts of employees, which as a practical matter are sure to occur in the conduct of the employer's enterprise, are placed upon that enterprise itself, as a required cost of doing business. They are placed upon the employer because, having engaged in an enterprise, which will on the basis of all past experience involve harm to others through the torts of employees, and sought to profit by it, it is just that he, rather than the innocent injured plaintiff, should bear them; because he is better able to absorb them, and to distribute them, through prices, rates or liability insurance, to the public, and so to shift them to society, to the community at large. Added to this is the makeweight argument that an employer who is strictly liable is under the greatest incentive to be careful in the selection, instruction and supervision of his servants, and to take every precaution to see that the enterprise is conducted safely.

Supervision is essential to risk management and successful business operations. It is a function of which mental health professionals approve in spirit, and yet they often do not accomplish it consistently or adequately. The old adage about good intentions can be rephrased: "The hallways to the malpractice courtrooms are carpeted with good intentions." Many of the principles for supervising professionals (described in the following section) are also applicable to the supervision of support staff members. Supervision must start when the support staff member crosses the threshold of the clinic, and it must continue with consistency and authority throughout his or her residency.

Supervision of Professional Associates

The "master-servant" principle and the related *Respondeat Superior* rule apply also to the professionals in the mental health practice group. Imputed or vicarious liability can extend to professional peers, as well as to the CEO. This makes it possible for the attorney of a client who alleges malpractice to name, for example, all members of the practice group as defendants, on the basis of duty to supervise. Thus, the plaintiff may allege that because the members of the practice group benefited from their affiliation, particularly in a financial manner, each had a duty to do everything possible to safeguard the public (the clients) from damage by an errant member of the practice group. Certainly, if a client had been served by several members (for example, a psychologist did the testing, a social worker did the psychotherapy, and a psychiatrist provided consultation to both of them), the principle of vicarious liability could lead to all three professionals' being held liable for the wrongdoing of only one.

As already mentioned, good intentions are not enough to make supervision materialize, nor does actual supervision always fulfill good intentions:

> Even for the competent supervisor, there are only so many hours in the day, and the professional has only so much energy. An overload of, say, clinical cases can lead the harried mental health professional to neglect the supervision that is essential to risk management. It will be necessary either to balance commitments to accommodate the supervisory objective or to designate the responsibility to

> someone else . . . no matter who is appointed, the entire organization (including associated professionals and nonprofessionals) must show a readiness to let the supervisor supervise. Some professionals are resistant to uncovering their performance to a supervisor (or even to a colleague). Regardless of seniority, it is never beneath the dignity of a professional to receive supervision. In fact, the professional who seeks supervision should be viewed as mature, well trained, and self-assured; the professional who avoids supervision ("With all my training, I don't need any more supervision—I know what to do!") should be viewed as defensive, poorly trained, and self-doubting. This person is also a high-risk associate [Woody, 1988b, p. 98].

The mental health CEO is responsible for preparing the organization to accept and support supervisory efforts. While supervision can be provided by an in-house source, such as a senior colleague (perhaps the CEO), there will be distinct benefits for group dynamics and risk management if someone from outside the group practice provides the supervision. An outside supervisor probably has the best chance of minimizing defensiveness, overcoming interpersonal barriers (caused by nonsupervisory interactions within the organization), and gaining optimal communication openness and behavioral compliance. Moreover, in the event of a lawsuit, testimony from a supervisor who is not a member of the practice group will probably impress a judge or jury as more objective than what might be viewed as self-serving testimony from a supervisor who is also a member of the group practice.

Entrepreneurship in mental health services requires astute management of human resources. Without a doubt, the end product, as measured by quality of service, depends on the characteristics of professional and support staff members. Group dynamics are subject to leadership and management (for example, a sense of shared responsibility for obtaining business objectives can be developed). For all intents and purposes, human resources constitute the primary asset of a mental health practice group. Consequently, nothing can be left to chance, presumed, or taken for granted. There must be a systemic perspective on influence and control. Selection of personnel must be dictated by their competence, and their retention must be supported by training. Even for the CEO, as well as for everyone else, supervision is essential to maximizing contributions toward the success of the business.

CHAPTER 7

Managing Operations: Practical Aspects of Running an Office

ONCE THE MENTAL HEALTH BUSINESS IS UNDER WAY, the challenge becomes effective management. Business planning is a prerequisite, but the old adage "The best laid plans oftimes go astray" applies here. The management of operations provides the means to achieve the goals that were conceptualized during the planning and marketing phases (although those two phases will always continue during operations).

Effective management of operations has many facets. Technically, it means acquiring space, equipment, and supplies, as necessary. In terms of resources, it means recruiting, selecting, training, and retaining persons to be support staff members. The operations will also be important to the management of the professionals associated with the mental health practice. Procedurally, it means setting up data systems, such as for bookkeeping, client information (accounts and records), collections, and disbursements (including those to creditors). In terms of risk management, it means having all the operations compatible with ethical considerations and legally appropriate standards.

The business plan should address all foreseeable aspects of operations. This section of the business plan constitutes an "operations plan," and covers requirements for "space, equipment, labor, geographic issues . . . overhead issues, [and] transfer payments" (Pinchot, 1985, p. 133). Even so, there will always be considerable subjectivity present in the judgments made by the mental health CEO, and the purpose of this chapter is to provide an overview of issues and options in the management of operations.

Selecting, Outfitting, and Designing the Office

There is no simple criterion for selecting an office. The business plan will address space needs, as determined by present and future personnel and services. Every mental health entrepreneur must cope with the fact that office space usually involves a contractual obligation, such as a lease for a period of years or a purchase agreement for ownership of the space, and if a different location or amount of space becomes desirable for some reason, it may be difficult both to relocate and to increase or decrease the amount of one's office space.

Contractual Considerations. Whether space is obtained through a rental or leasing agreement or through a purchase, it is wise to build in as many escape routes as possible. For example, an office building might be rented for a short term, with an option to buy at a later date (with, perhaps, some of the rent applied toward the purchase price). In fashioning a rental or leasing agreement, it is sometimes possible to get the lessor (the landlord) to agree that, with a substantial amount of lead time, the lessee (the mental health CEO) can move to other (larger or smaller) space owned or managed by the lessor or can terminate the agreement because of the lessee's unilateral determination of need. Another option is to have a clause that allows the agreement to be unilaterally terminated by the lessee if he or she moves the mental health practice to another locale (say, a certain number of miles from the present site). Many lessors are open to this option, especially if the lessee agrees to the right's being predicated on substantial notice, to allow the lessor to find another lessee.

A major concern is that the practice may not yield enough money to meet bills or stay in business. This should be a pragmatic concern to lessor and lessee alike. If the mental health CEO has accepted a certain form of business entity, it may be possible to avoid personal liability for, say, rental payments if the practice folds. Depending on the laws of the particular state, it may be possible to avoid personal liability if the agreement is signed "for the Corporation." Of course, savvy lessors are aware of corporate versus personal liability and may push to have agreements signed "personally and for the Corporation."

Also depending on the laws of the particular jurisdiction, the breach of a rental or leasing agreement usually leaves the lessee responsible for the lessor's lost income. For example, if the mental health practice failed, the CEO might have to pay rent for the remainder of the agreement, but the lessor would probably be required to make a good-faith effort to rent or lease the space to another lessee, to mitigate damages. If the lessor could not find a replacement for the lessee, or if the replacement lessee paid less, the difference in the lessor's income would be the burden of the original lessee.

No one ever expects not to be able to work throughout the entire term of a rental or leasing agreement. Nevertheless, the death or disability of the mental health CEO (or of key associates) could leave a heavy financial burden—say, on the estate. At the negotiation stage, the lessee should posit a clause that would terminate the duty to pay upon death or disability (defined).

The flexibility of lessors depends, as might be expected, on personal temperament and on the market availability of competitive space. Clearly, these factors are variable. The property's management may move to another agent, ushering in new interpersonal dynamics, or the economic conditions of the locale can shift because of over- or underavailability of comparable space.

The professional who is negotiating a rental or leasing agreement should remember that the document was written by the lessor's attorney and therefore contains terms favorable to the lessor, such as those that stipulate who will pay for liability insurance, or what will happen in the event of a fire or a natural disaster. Special attention should be devoted to obtaining well-defined terms for any issue or condition that may involve

money, such as for those that stipulate who will pay for re-
modeling that meets the needs of the lessee and improves the
value of the property for the lessor. Even if the document is a
preprinted form (perhaps purchased at an office-supply store),
there are versions of forms that are tailored to the preferences of
the lessor. Whatever the preprinted form, it can be modified.
The mental health CEO should be prepared to exercise his or
her psychological skills of persuasion, negotiation, and personal
relations to obtain unique terms suited to and supportive of the
business plan. (Retyping a long, preprinted lease form to include special terms and conditions can be well worth the secretarial costs.)

Space. Selection of space should be determined by the business
plan, rather than by impetuous decisions or serendipitous
choices. People can succumb to exhilarating rushes of self-
importance or vanity. One mental health CEO, who was quite
successful in his overall planning and marketing, met financial
ruin through his faulty selection of space. He erroneously assumed that clients would be willing to pay higher fees for service if the mental health practice were located in the "high-rent
district." For his two offices, he purchased a condominium in a
medical park for a premium price and, perhaps even worse
(since he could presumably sell the condominium, even if at a
loss), he signed a ten-year lease for a suite of offices on an upper
floor of a high-priced building. His rationale was "My clients
will love this view." His clients did like coming to a prestigious
medical complex for treatment, and they did enjoy the pan-
oramic view from the high-rise suite. By most business standards,
the cash flow was very good, but it was not good enough to
meet the overhead incurred through the exorbitant expense for
office space. Despite his strong clinical skills and his usually
wise management, this mental health CEO ended up declaring
bankruptcy.
    The business plan will be based on analyses of what loca-
tions will best further the enterprise, with due consideration
given to financial reality. At the most general level, selecting the
city where the practice will be requires personal preferences to

be blended with the business plan and market analyses. At a more specific level, determining the exact location in the city will depend primarily on the elements of the business plan, such as its marketing and financial factors.

When a mental health practice is in an urban area, clients seem to seek services within a reasonable driving distance; that is, a client is not likely to drive across town to receive service that is obtainable nearby, unless there is a special reason to do so. An exception may be made, however, for a practitioner with an outstanding reputation, specialized service, or referrals from a particular source, and for these reasons, clients may travel substantial distances. For example, in a state with very few well-trained sex therapists, one sex therapist is surprised by the number of clients who live long distances from her office yet arrive for weekly appointments. A neuropsychologist receives referrals from neurologists in other cities. A forensic psychologist provides expert testimony to clients all over the United States. For such clients as these, the section of the city where the office is has little importance. All things being equal, however, the decision on where to locate should reflect the types of clients to whom the clinical services will be marketed.

The financial status of the preferred client must be considered. If the practice is tailored to clients who have the ability to pay top dollar for high-quality service, it is illogical to locate the office in an undesirable section of the city. At the same time, simply wanting financially able clients does not mean that they will be available; they probably constitute one of the most competitive market sectors. Unless the mental health group, on the basis of its market analysis, concludes that it can successfully compete for the financially affluent sector, locating in a "high-rent district" may be ill advised. A psychiatrist and a psychologist purposely chose an office in a decaying part of town because they knew that the bulk of their clients were supported by meager public rehabilitation funding and consequently lived nearby.

When a mental health practice is in a rural area, the situation is apt to be different. To reach an adequate number of potential clients, the catchment area must be geographically wide. The types of clients will also tend to be more diverse. In a rural area, it would be most fruitful to serve clients from a broad spectrum of socioeconomic backgrounds, and specialization would be more difficult.

The neighborhood and the building in which the mental health practice is situated must fulfill the expectations of clients. The person receiving services expects to be treated with dignity. Such treatment is, of course, most evident in the demeanor of the professionals and the support staff members, but it is also aided by the environment. Therefore, in general, it is desirable for the mental health practice to be in a neighborhood and/or in a building that contains other professional services.

Is being near potential referral sources (say, particular physicians and attorneys) necessary? On the one hand, the best referrals usually result from interpersonal communication (see Chapter Four), not proximity. On the other hand, the propinquity concept (which has been documented by extensive social-psychological research) holds that physical closeness promotes attraction. According to Worchel and Cooper (1983, p. 267), "the more frequently individuals had seen each other, the more they chose to interact with, and discuss personal details with, each other." More referrals may be obtained through propinquity, and there is the expectation that further interactions are expected, or even unavoidable.

Mobley, Elkins, and Mobley (1987/88, p. 67), writing for psychiatrists, say: "Two factors are important in site selection: (1) the site should be convenient enough for psychiatrists with respect to hospital commuting, and (2) the site should accommodate the patient's sense of privacy. Other aspects of office location that merit consideration are the expense of the location, adequate parking facilities, the square footage of the office facility, suitable waiting areas, and possible facilities for group therapy. The importance of each of these factors may vary with the objectives of the practice." Regardless of the particular mental health discipline, the decision about the amount of space needed will depend largely on the exact services to be offered. For example, a certain practitioner may not require a group room; another may need smaller rooms for psychological assessment or biofeedback training. The decision will also reflect the extent to which the practice is present- versus future-oriented. Realistically, the mental health CEO should consider probable growth-related needs and yet rely on current known income (with the possibility of space reduction or expansion due to unforeseen circumstances).

Unnecessary expenditures commonly result from overestimation of the amount of space needed for a waiting room. While esthetics and spaciousness are important to the office atmosphere, there is also the pragmatic question of how much space is actually required to comfortably accommodate the number of persons who are likely to be present at any one time. If the mental health practice provides family therapy, the waiting room will probably be larger than if the practice emphasizes individual therapy or psychodiagnostics. Having toilets in the rented or leased space instead of in a common area may also elevate costs.

Consideration must also be given to special space needs. For example, the psychodiagnostician accumulates a lot of client records, and space will be needed for storage. Special equipment, such as computers, also require space. Support staff members must have room to work efficiently. Good morale is a good reason for a staff lounge where professionals and support staff members can get away from work, even if only for a few minutes. Laws at all levels usually already prescribe accessibility for handicapped persons, but the mental health CEO should still consider these special needs when selecting space. For example, elevators may be necessary, and hallways and doorways should be wide enough for wheelchairs.

The unique nature of mental health services creates special design and space issues. Some practitioners prefer to distance themselves from clients, perhaps by having a private restroom or a private entrance. If several solo or independent practitioners share a suite or building and wish to create an impression of independence from one another (for business and/or risk-management purposes), the design may also entail separate entrances or waiting areas for clients. In one malpractice case, the issue of possible vicarious liability hinged, in part, on the fact that practitioner A, the alleged wrongdoer, had a separate entrance for his clients but nevertheless allowed them to enter through practitioner B's doorway and lobby. The liability question was whether this entrance arrangement created a reasonable belief in the mind of the plaintiff-client that the two practitioners were in a group practice and that, consequently, they had the implied duty to supervise or be responsible for each other's standard of care.

The need to ensure the confidentiality of therapists' and clients' verbal interactions must also be accommodated by design and space. The least expensive alternatives are to purchase an electronic apparatus that uses "white noise" to disrupt vocal soundwaves or to install a music system to override voices that otherwise could be heard though partitions. If the space needs partitions, the design and construction may involve separating the inner and outer walls by attaching each layer of drywall (on each side of the partition) to its own stud (double-studding) and stuffing the space between with insulation or another sound retardant. Less major renovations can include using two doors (one opening into the office, and one opening onto the hallway) or packing overhead space with insulation or another sound retardant. In any event, confidentiality is essential to effective therapeutic interventions, and spending money to ensure confidentiality is an essential business expenditure.

There will probably come a time—perhaps because of success and the need for more space—when a move is in order. Planning and follow-up arrangements should ensure that a move goes smoothly. In moving it is necessary to ensure that clients' records will remain confidential; set a moving date that will allow for minimal interruption of service; notify past, present, and potential clients and referral sources of the impending move; prepare the new office space with installations, fixtures, and furnishings in a timely manner, to minimize the interruption of service; and plan for a host of other details (Young, 1988).

Furnishings. Many of the considerations for selecting space apply to outfitting the office. The tendency to overspend for the sake of an image—supposedly to further marketing goals by impressing clients—may actually be rooted in self-aggrandizement and must be resisted. Since communications and data processing are crucial to success, telephones, computers, typewriters, photocopy machines, telecopiers, test-scoring scanners, and related equipment deserve high priority. Nevertheless, expenditures should be restricted to what is necessary and practical.

The type of mental health service will determine priorities for acquiring equipment. For example, a psychodiagnostician may require a computer, a scanner, and/or a telecopier for scoring and interpreting tests at a remote facility, while a marriage and family therapist may have little or no use for such equipment. Furniture should be selected according to its functions. To be sure, high-quality furniture, such as leather-covered chairs, may contribute positively to the tone of the office; at the same time, however, the comfort of a client who is seated for a straight fifty minutes of therapy is probably more important than mere appearance. The mental health CEO should authorize the acquisition of furnishings that will be justified by their performance. New pieces of furniture should be added according to plan and need, not because they are available or affordable at the moment.

Office Design. The structure and design of the office and its workstations should derive from the tasks that will be performed. Professional architects and office designers, of course, can provide useful expertise. They can perform objective analyses of movements, tasks, and so on, to create a physical layout that will maximize efficiency and productivity for the operational system. With or without expert opinion, however, certain barriers to smooth operations should be readily discernible. One practitioner recognized that when he prepared correspondence, he did each letter or envelope on the word processor, got up and walked across the room to the storage area and picked up a single sheet of paper or a single envelope, printed the item, wrote the next piece of correspondence, got up and walked across the room to the storage area, and so forth. By investing in a stationery rack that could be mounted on the wall over his desk, he enhanced his work flow.

In new buildings, it is not uncommon for a lessee to be responsible for partitioning the leased or rented space. It is important to have a careful layout that eliminates any wasted space. For this seemingly simple task, help from an architect or sometimes even from a knowledgeable carpenter will yield functional dividends.

Hiring Support Staff Members

Any action, whether of omission or commission, by a support staff member potentially imposes liability on the mental health CEO, and perhaps on other associates as well (see Chapter Six). If an employee causes damage to another person or to property, the remedy may be at the expense of the employer. The employer has a duty to make a reasonable effort to ensure that all persons associated with the business endeavor meet an acceptable standard of care. If an employee operating within his or her job definition or "scope of duty" causes injury to someone, the employer is likely to be liable for the damages; the employer is reasoned to be in control of the employee's acts.

Public policy often imposes higher standards on certain types of businesses, such as railroads and airlines, hotels and motels, and health-care providers, because these kinds of businesses control the conditions for safety and welfare of consumers. Thus, responsibility for protection clearly falls to the business that stands to profit from the service.

Risk management demands that employees' training be adequate for their jobs. For example, mental health practitioners know they must protect the confidentiality and privileged communications of clients. A layperson who has just joined a group practice in a supporting role, however, may not understand this principle and its rationale. Therefore, he or she needs training, and there must be an ongoing system for supervising and monitoring the support staff member's adherence to the standard of care. (More will be said on supervision in Chapter Eight.)

Selecting an Accountant and an Attorney

To operate any business successfully (and the mental health business is certainly no exception), the CEO must have access to the expertise of ancillary professionals. They are critical allies for planning, problem solving, and risk management. For the mental health CEO, two important kinds of allies are accountants and attorneys.

Accountants. Tax laws make accurate and effective bookkeeping a legal requirement, but it is also much more. Bookkeeping involves both records and documentation: "When we use the term *documentation,* we are generally speaking of the method you use to prove your legitimate tax deductions, credits, or other tax benefits" (Bradford and Davis, 1984, p. 9). Keeping an activity log can document tax figures (say, the percentage of business use of an automobile or home telephone) and provide for risk management (for example, by proving what services were provided to a client). Careful financial records provide data crucial to analysis, which in turn is needed for business planning and marketing. Support staff members will play a day-to-day role in these matters, but it may also be necessary to acquire the services of an outside accountant, one with special expertise.

In selecting outside accountants, it is logical to consider their training and other qualifications. A certified public accountant (CPA) has proven his or her academic competence by examination. There are also many accountants who lack this proof of competence yet are highly knowledgeable and skilled. As Bradford and Davis (1984, p. 27) point out, "A tax *advisor* is not simply a tax return *preparer.* A preparer takes the numbers you provide and fills out your tax return. A tax advisor helps you run your tax life in a way that will produce numbers favorable to you." Since a support staff member can typically be trained to keep records and prepare books for documentation purposes, the message is straightforward: The prudent mental health CEO must have adequate consultation from a tax adviser. Accountants can provide three types of (fiscal) year-end statements (Baty, 1981, p. 110):

1. *Unaudited.* These statements, even though they be prepared by your auditor, have little

weight with outside persons, because they are
merely prepared from the books of account
without benefit of auditing.

2. *Audited, Uncertified.* These statements are the
    result of a partial audit, in which most but not
    all of the steps may have been taken. For ex-
    ample, it may be that the auditor was unable
    to witness the taking of inventory, although
    the other tests have been performed.

3. *Certified.* This is the most believable, because
    it means that all steps have been taken, and
    the auditing firm has stuck its neck out as far
    as possible.

The mental health CEO facing a fiscal problem (expenditures or
taxes) should select from these three qualitative levels according
to his or her need. For financial reasons, it may be best to rely
on an in-house, unaudited compilation and analysis, or turn to a
neighborhood accountant. If the stakes are high, it may be
necessary to use the services of a well-established public accounting firm; the biggest ones have offices in many locations.
(Costs and personalized service always must be considered.)

An auditor has a powerful role and is called into service
for major financial reasons—to place a value on the mental health
practice for resale, to resolve a dispute between partners, to deal
with tax questions. It is not an easygoing affair:

> The auditing firm you select is your big friend—un-
> til the day of your first audit. From that point for-
> ward they may seem to become your adversary.
> They will criticize your cash control system, will
> wish to create reserves for bad debts in excess of
> anything you can imagine, and also to reserve for
> specific accounts which may be a bit slow in col-
> lecting . . . . They will find your cost accounting in-
> adequate to determine the actual labor and materials
> content of your work-in-process. They will want
> you to write off your capitalized development

costs. They will discover that a couple of your accounts receivable claim never to have seen an invoice from your firm. In short, they will appear to be doing everything possible to reduce your bottom line profit, for which you have labored so long and hard" [Baty, 1981, pp. 111–112].

Nevertheless, an auditor, as "devil's advocate," can stimulate new thought and insight. Since the outside accountant is working for the mental health CEO, the provocative advice can be accepted or rejected.

Selecting an accountant is not easy. Bradford and Davis (1984, p. 28) recommend choosing a tax adviser who specializes in "the tax problems of psychiatrists and other professionals," but they acknowledge the difficulty of finding one "whose *only* clients are psychiatrists or other doctors." What is important is that the mental health CEO have a trusted accountant with whom he or she communicates well and who provides adequate information for accounting decisions. At all stages, from planning to operating, the mental health business must be conducted according to sound accounting principles.

Attorneys. It is common to think of attorneys' services from a risk-management perspective. Unquestionably, a mental health practitioner who is facing an ethical, regulatory, or legal complaint should turn the matter over to an attorney and rely heavily on the attorney's expertise. But legal consultation is also an important part of the effective management of operations. All kinds of issues—type of business entity, policies for managing the practice, approaches to selecting and promoting staff members, taxation, investment opportunities, and a host of other routine matters—have legal consequences.

As in selecting an accountant, selecting an attorney entails decisions. Ideally, the mental health CEO should have an attorney who is familiar with business law for mental health disciplines. An attorney who usually performs only one type of legal service—say, divorces or real-estate transactions—may or may not also know about the business issues of mental health practice. Moreover, the mental health professional who is being sued for malpractice needs legal support different from what would be useful for day-to-day business operations. Like any other consultant, an attorney should be someone whom the CEO can trust and communicate with and who provides information adequate to guide legal decisions. The entrepreneur geared toward astute business planning, decision making, and circumvention of problems needs reliable legal information.

Relying on Teamwork. In Chapters Two and Three, considerable attention was devoted to the benefits available from drawing colleagues (professional and support staff members) into the mental health business planning and operations; more will be said on this matter in Chapter Eight. Equally important, the mental health business team must have an accountant and an attorney available, even if on a "pinch hitter" basis.

In helping mental health professionals protect their practices, it is perplexing to find widespread naïveté about the business and risk-management benefits that can be obtained through the specialized expertise of an accountant and an attorney. It may simply be a lack of understanding, left unattended by the nonbusiness orientation of university training. It may be a personal reluctance to set aside the outdated social service model, with its emphasis on altruism, and to adopt the modern health-care business model, with its emphasis on standard of care and business acumen. If it is the former, it can presumably be remedied by the practitioner's having an open mind to contemporary information. If it is the latter, the clinging to the past will manifest a blind spot to the need to invest funds in the right places. In any number of lawsuits, it is common to have the plaintiff-client's attorney recognize a mental health practitioner's business-related bungling and say, in effect, "Doesn't the doctor recognize the costs of doing business?" While the crass statement is offensive, it has a ring of truth. Regretfully, it does seem as if too many mental health practitioners have an unwise view about trying to minimize business expenses, even if the thriftiness creates unnecessary risk or jeopardizes business success.

It should be clear that the mental health CEO is typically

not qualified to provide answers to accounting and legal questions. While prudent spending is a hallmark of successful business, there is a point where it is foolish to fail to invest funds in essential ancillary expertise, such as from an accountant and attorney. These services should be viewed as reasonable and necessary expenditures for the operations of the mental health business. The Internal Revenue Service recognizes payments for these services in this light, allowing them to be deducted as business expenses. Certainly, the successful mental health CEO will recognize the benefits that can be derived from accounting and legal services.

Managing Accounts

Client accounts sustain the mental health business. For whatever reason, a goodly number of mental health professionals have trouble accepting the notion of a client's being obligated to pay for services. No doubt, much of this reluctance is a throwback to the days when mental health services were embraced by public policy as being a social service, and the foremost benefit to the practitioner was often mistakenly presumed to be altruistic reward. In those days (especially during the Kennedy and Johnson administrations, in the 1960s), there were public funds available to subsidize human services. Rightly or wrongly, current public policy has lessened tax support for social and human services and has placed mental health services into the health-care industry (as discussed in Chapter One). Now mental health services are supported by the exchange theory: Two parties provide each other with a benefit; the client needs treatment and, in exchange for it, must pay the mental health practitioner.

Educating the Client to the Financial Obligation. It is important that the client be educated to his or her financial obligations. Part of the standard intake procedure should include providing a written statement of the financial terms to each client and to significant others (parents or spouse, who may have some financial connection during treatment). As mentioned in Chapter Six, either the service brochure or a separate document can present financial information. To create a legal obligation it is not necessary to have the client sign an agreement on the financial terms (although a signed document is not precluded); as long as the routine business procedure includes providing clients with particular information (and a support staff member can testify accordingly), acceptance of service evidences implicit agreement to the financial terms. (Of course, it should be noted in the client's records when financial issues were specified and discussed.)

Although it is not mandatory, a written contract can be useful. If a contract is used, care should be taken to avoid any connotation of a guaranteed outcome of treatment. There should certainly be no touting of the service as being superior in quality. At the same time, there should be no attempt to avoid meeting a reasonable standard of care. It would probably be unconscionable to attempt to circumvent liability—for example, by asking a client to waive liability ahead of time. In the event of a legal action, such a maneuver could work to the detriment of the practitioner. The contract should spell out the terms of services and fees, how payments can be made, any special charges, any interest that will be attached, and third-party payments. (Each of these issues will be discussed later in detail.)

Motivating a Client to Pay. A fundamental of motivating a client to meet a financial obligation is to keep him or her fully informed about the status of the account. Too often, the mental health practitioner may consciously reason: "I'd better not talk about the overdue debt; that may be a therapeutic setback." On the contrary, failure to deal with an overdue debt is to court avoidance of responsibility. For other client management and service areas, the practitioner does not hesitate to confront the client with reality, so as to help the person deal with life. The practitioner's reason for not dealing directly with account issues may be his or her unconscious conflict about competence and charging for the service. Part of keeping the client informed is to talk readily and openly about payments made or owed.

A special policy is needed for sessions that are missed or

cancelled at the last minute. Missed sessions are troubling for both the client and the practitioner: If a client fails to show up for an appointment, the client suffers from lack of treatment, and the practitioner suffers from lack of income. With other than unavoidable emergencies, the client's inability to keep an appointment or to cancel or reschedule it in a timely manner should be recognized for what it reflects, and the practitioner should not be required to suffer because of the client's shortcomings. Therefore, the financial policy on this issue should be clear. It seems reasonable to say that the client will be billed and expected to pay for any scheduled session that is missed and not cancelled at least twenty-four hours beforehand. For tardy cancellations or unavoidable absences, the practitioner will make a good-faith effort to schedule a replacement appointment, but if this cannot be accomplished, the client will be responsible for full payment. Note: Missed sessions cannot be billed to third-party insurance carriers.

A system should be in place for regularly billing the client. Too often, the mental health practitioner (especially if he or she is in solo practice) follows the unwise practice of irregular or occasional billing. To obtain a steady and predictable cash flow requires an established billing procedure; these are basic effective management operations. A good means of achieving regularity and confrontation is to have a bill prepared for the client at the end of every appointment.

Clients' motivation is also furthered by an occasional progress report (O'Bryan, 1988). Many a mental health client has dropped out of treatment because of flagging incentive. With a personalized letter (which is not in itself solicitous), the practitioner can emphasize the benefits that have been and will be gained. This encourages the client to continue in treatment and, of course, impliedly to make payments.

Determining the Professional Fee. The old flip response— "Charge what you can get away with"—is inappropriate to determining a professional fee. Rather, the fee should be based on an integration of three factors: the competence of the professional, the expenses associated with the operations, and what the market will support. (Note that a criterion is *not* "what the client can afford to pay." More will be said later about *pro bono* service.)

One wag has said, in effect, "I find out what the highest-paid mental health professional, regardless of discipline, in the community charges, and then I charge five dollars per hour more!" That idea may sound enticing, and it caters to the notion that clients benefit from believing that the professional must be good because the fee is higher than what other practitioners charge. While there is some research support for that idea, there is also contradictory evidence: The fee can serve as a positive motivator, but the amount can also become a negative factor. In other words, practitioners can price themselves right out of business. At the same time, charging a fee that is too low can produce the same undesirable result.

It is logical for expertise to be the primary determinant of fee. The more skill, the higher the fee. Unfortunately, the market does not always ensure a return on advanced training. In a profession, there is a threshold amount of training (for example, the "terminal" degree, and licensure for the discipline), and anything beyond may serve the practitioner's interest in a specialized practice or in personal edification but yield little financial payoff.

Pragmatism demands concern about overhead costs. If the business plan has been wisely constructed, the operating expenses must be accommodated by the professional fee. One practitioner lamented how, despite her carefully prepared business plan and efficient management system, the overhead, which would have been reasonable elsewhere, ended up being exorbitant in comparison to fee-generated income. In that particular community, about one-third of the county's population consisted of retirees who wanted considerable service, yet clients from this group could not afford services that were not covered fully by Medicare. Operating expenses must be based on accurate projections of fees, including the client's ability to pay the total fee and the likelihood of a client's having health-care insurance that will make a partial payment for service.

The amount of competition will also affect the amount

of the professional fee. In a locale with little or no governmental regulation (that is, no licensure) of mental health disciplines other than psychology and psychiatry, the availability of services from unlicensed practitioners may require psychologists and psychiatrists to keep their fees relatively low. The consumer wants good quality and is sometimes willing to pay for services from a psychologist or a psychiatrist, rather than from practitioners in other mental disciplines—especially if third-party (insurance) payments are available only for services provided by psychologists and psychiatrists. Nevertheless, cost may lead the consumer to accept an unregulated service, even if its quality is not ensured through licensure.

Logging Services. Within professional services management, it is known that many practitioners lack systematic means of recording every service that could appropriately be charged for. In mental health services, the most glaring omission in recording is the fee charged for indirect services, such as a telephone conference with another health-care provider (say, the client's family physician) or an attorney. In each instance, the only reason for the conference was to benefit the client. Another omission in recording involves telephone conferences with clients. Scheduling and rescheduling appointments aside, any other advice or information is intended to benefit the client, and the mental health practitioner deserves payment.

There is a simple and academically sound formula (which some of my clients have dubbed the Woody Rule): If the communication or service (1) relies on the expertise of the professional, (2) is intended to benefit the client, and (3) creates potential ethical, regulatory, or legal liability for the practitioner, a professional fee is justified. In fact, this litigious era leads to liability for virtually anything that is done or should have been done by a mental health practitioner. Consequently, information provided to or exchanged with, say, a physician or an attorney is definitely cloaked in the confidentiality (and other protections) of professionalism, and liability attaches. Likewise, a telephone call from a client must be dealt with according to professional standards, including taking notes, even (perhaps especially) if the call is taken outside the office, and liability attaches. Failure to use this approach to billing is self-denigrating and is not good business.

This three-factored rule for charging should not be applied to a client without notice. It can, however, be discussed in the service brochure provided to a client and significant others. If presented in a straightforward way at the outset of the professional relationship, the Woody Rule will, more likely than not, be readily accepted and will lead to improved income for the practitioner. There may also be another benefit for both the client and the practitioner: Being aware of the significance of every contact with the professional, the client will be pressed to self-responsibility, avoiding unnecessary and unhealthy reliance on the practitioner and, with fewer interruptions and pressures in his or her personal life, the practitioner may experience less stress and increased professional productivity.

None of the foregoing speaks against benevolence or altruism. Whether right or wrong in terms of social philosophy, all the comments about establishing and logging a professional fee have solid support in contemporary public policy, which regards mental health services as part of the health-care industry. Keep in mind that the mental health practitioner is legally liable, regardless of the amount of his or her fee (and even if no fee is attached to service).

There are opposing views. For example, the American Psychological Association (1981a, p. 636) declares that practitioners should "contribute a portion of their services to work for which they receive little or no financial return." There is some doubt that a professional association can impose sanctions for "unethical" conduct if a professional will not sacrifice his or her constitutionally protected right to pursue an occupation; nevertheless, urging psychologists and other mental health practitioners to help persons in need is intended for the benefit of society.

The professional can answer the call of social altruism by means other than providing free service or reducing fees to clients who allege that they cannot afford treatment. With diminished priority for public funding of mental health services, many persons who formerly would have qualified for publicly supported mental health services are left to their own devices. Too often, this situation is devastating, especially for the chronically mentally ill, who, without health-care support, drift into unhealthy and unsafe conditions on the street; they now number in the millions (Rossi, Wright, Fisher, and Willis, 1987). According to the American Psychological Association (1981a, p. 634), "Both practitioners and researchers are concerned with the development of such legal and quasi-legal regulations as best serve the public interest, and they work toward changing existing regulations that are not beneficial to the public interest." This provides a call to psychologists, and it is equally directed to members of the other mental health disciplines, to be devoted to social action. Therefore, instead of feeling ethically or morally obligated to fulfill social service by free or reduced-fee arrangements for clinical services, the practitioner might better aid society and persons in need by aggressive efforts to shape public policy toward providing funding for mental health services. In addition to efforts to shape public policy, the practitioner may choose to volunteer services, such as to a poorly funded agency. When this is done, clients and society are benefited and the practitioner receives personal gratification. In this context, volunteerism is for a healthy social purpose, not a remedy for faulty business practice.

Making Payments. To increase the potential gross revenue, a practitioner may be tempted to take any client who will make even a halfhearted pledge to pay for service. This is ill advised. First, it may prove detrimental to the client. The client who clearly cannot afford the professional fee will be in conflict, and he or she will be unlikely to experience more than minimal benefits. Second, it is a foolish business judgment. Much effort—and therefore money—will be expended on trying to collect overdue debts. Further, it is well established that debtors try to avoid paying. With the mental health client, especially in this litigious era, the focus may quickly shift to what the practitioner did or should have done during the provision of service, as well as to what might justify an ethical, regulatory, or legal complaint: "There is ample evidence that as a deficit in payment rises, so too the likelihood of a malpractice claim rises" (Woody, 1988a, p. 122).

The preferred approach, even if the gross revenue turns out to be less, is to adhere to a "pay as we go" policy. Before treatment is initiated, third-party payments should be documented, and arrangements should be made for the client to pay the unreimbursed portion as treatment is provided. One mental health CEO stated, "If I tell clients from the beginning that they have to pay the unreimbursed portion as treatment is provided, I will lose clients." That may be true, but an important construct for the successful mental health business is having the right kind of client. Therefore, it is best to provide services only to clients who can and will fulfill their financial duties.

In the event that a debt is allowed, it should be by written agreement, with the payment arrangement clearly specified. If the client breaches the agreement, the issue should be discussed at the next encounter (or perhaps over the telephone beforehand). If the cost of treatment becomes an undue burden on the client, it is best (for the client's therapeutic benefit) to hold to a contract (the client needs to learn responsibility in decision making). If no immediate remedy is possible, it is to the benefit of client and practitioner alike to consider termination or referral to less expensive treatment. For the sake of risk management, there should be no negative emotions or abrupt abandonment; rather, the practitioner can choose to implement a no-fee arrangement during the interim between termination and the client's resuming treatment with another practitioner.

The foregoing policy is preferable from the standpoint of risk management and effective business, but the mental health CEO can also develop other policies. Credit cards can be accepted, or a long-term payment arrangement—with monthly interest—can be implemented by written contract. If the latter is chosen, the payments should exceed the amount of interest and be high enough to effectively reduce the balance due. Keep in mind, however, that a payment contract will not necessarily reduce or eliminate the client's consideration of flaws or faults in the service. Any manner of carrying accounts receivable continues the risk of a client's considering an ethical, regulatory, or legal action.

Reliance on third-party payments should involve direct documentation from the insurance carrier before treatment begins, or at least during the first few professional contacts. For the sake of risk management, it is important to avoid a buildup of the client's debt, and under no circumstances should the unreimbursed portion of the debt be overlooked. On deposition in a malpractice case, one mental health practitioner admitted to increasing his fee for clients who had health insurance (thereby assuring himself of receiving his regular amount via the portion paid by the insurance carrier) and telling his clients that he would make no effort to collect the amount that they would otherwise owe. While this blunder was just one of a whole constellation of actions that resulted in that particular practitioner's loss of his license, it is widely known that many mental health practitioners are more concerned about the third-party payment than they are about having the client pay the unreimbursed portion. The appropriate way of dealing with the unreimbursed portion, even though it is only a small part of the total bill, is to make a reasonable effort to collect it. To do otherwise is to teach the client a lesson in sociopathy.

Collecting Debts. In collecting a bad debt, the mental health practitioner has the same legal entitlement and procedures as any other creditor. For example, the client who fails to pay for professional services has no right to the confidentiality that might be supposed to preclude the practitioner's asking a collection agency to pursue payment. Likewise, there can be a remedy through a court of law. The so-called small claims court affords a simple and inexpensive option (although some jurisdictions will not allow an attorney to represent the creditor, and the maximum amount is fixed). For larger amounts of money, other courts are available. A court judgment can be transformed, depending on the jurisdiction, into a garnishment of wages or a lien on property.

In this discussion, the important point is twofold. First, the mental health CEO should develop an effective debt-collection policy for the practice. This policy must be fashioned with legal counsel (since jurisdictions vary greatly on debt-related legal issues), clients should be informed accordingly, and the operations should consistently maintain the policy. Second, even with legal remedies available, it may be unwise to pursue debt collection. As mentioned previously, attempts to collect a debt from a mental health client—even if it is a valid debt predicated on a detailed agreement approved in advance by the client— can lead the client to consider means of avoiding payment, and his or her thoughts may turn to ethical, regulatory, and legal complaints. Keep in mind that the perception of some clients, by virtue of their mental health problems, may be prone to distortion, and what the mental health practitioner remembers as having actually happened during treatment may sound very different from a client's emotionally conflicted allegations to an attorney.

When a client refuses to pay a valid debt (especially when he or she is known to have the money), it is easy to take personal offense. Instead, what is needed is professional defense. Just as entrepreneurship does not allow tradition for tradition's sake, it does not allow emotion for emotion's sake. Prudent calculations of risk and investments must be made.

Given the relationship between debt and litigiousness, the mental health CEO should carefully consider what the costs might be for pursuing a legal remedy. Among other things, the client who is sued is surely going to tell others, and word will circulate throughout the community. The gossip will probably not be taken as a reflection of the client's irresponsibility but will emphasize the practitioner's uncaring pursuit of the almighty dollar, even against the mentally vulnerable. Referrals could drop off. Payments to a collection agency or to an attorney (or simply the cost of one's valuable time, which could be used to generate other income) will also lessen the net benefits of debt collection. Even if a judgment is received, it may be difficult to collect. If the client has no money, the judgment is apt to be worthless (depending on the jurisdiction, garnishment of wages is not always possible). An irresponsible client may be evasive, and it will be difficult to locate assets that could be subject to a lien. This is why it is a good idea to record the name and address of the bank and the account number for all checks received or, better yet, require the client to provide account numbers at the time of initial service.

There is often much more to be gained from collecting a bad debt than the money itself. Mental health practice should be conducted according to business principles, and business and risk-management principles contraindicate allowing any debt to accrue. Therefore, when a substantial debt has been built up and is large enough for the mental health CEO to conclude that the risk of a complaint is outweighed by the possible benefits of collection, he or she should think about why, given all the arguments against allowing debts to occur, this debt has reached this elevated amount. The answer may be painfully revealing of a conscious or unconscious motive on the part of the practitioner (countertransference, business ineptitude, or greed, for example).

Keeping Records

Records for clients serve many purposes. Originally, a record was conceptualized as being primarily for the benefit of the client. By making notes on what was done with the client, the practitioner was taking time to analyze the situation and evaluate alternatives for proceeding. Part of the structure of the record involved formulating an individualized treatment plan, documenting it (such as by psychological test data or clinical information), and monitoring progress. In another vein, if the client were later to see another health-care provider, the initial practitioner could forward the client's record, and the second practitioner could serve the client better by understanding what had been tried and learned during the earlier intervention. Such benefits to clients are still important.

Nowadays, however, the client record has also taken on two new meanings. First, the client record can be a source of data for business planning. Marketing plans can draw from what attracted previous and current clients to the practice and can extrapolate who future clients are apt to be and what services they will need. Second, the client record has critical importance for risk management. Since it documents what was and was not provided to the client, the record is usually the first piece of data analyzed by an attorney representing a potential litigant-client. Complaints to an ethics committee, a state regulatory agency, or a court commonly use the client record as the acid test of legitimacy for the claim.

It is beyond the scope of this discussion to present guidelines or forms for keeping client records; those can be found elsewhere (Kagle, 1984; Roach, Chernoff, and Esley, 1985; Waters and Murphy, 1979; Woody, 1988a, Woody, 1988b). For the management of operations, suffice it to say that the record should follow a standardized recording system, reflect an accurate log of the services and their purposes, and document everything that occurs. If the business plan has ordained certain constructs that will be evaluated periodically (such as for marketing objectives), contemporaneous recordings of the pertinent data should be made (avoiding any massive mounds of data that have to be sorted through at a later date). For risk management, it is especially important to document the standard of care (in Chapter Eight, more will be said about this matter), including the treatment plan, rationale, and monitoring. The practitioner should record the gist of all seemingly significant communications by the client, as well as by the practitioner (practitioners tend to enter clients' comments more than they do their own, even though lawsuits are based on what the practitioner said or did not say, and not on what the client said). Of course, records must be protected (for confidentiality) and preserved in a manner that will allow their ready retrieval.

Managing Clients

Effective operations require that clients adhere to policies and procedures. Similarly, risk management requires that clients adhere to treatment plans. In both areas, it is easier said than done. Perhaps because of the nature of their problems, mental health clients are infamous for nonadherence (such as failure to follow recommendations, and attrition from psychotherapeutic intervention; see Meichenbaum and Turk, 1987). Nonadherence has a significant negative effect on the service-delivery system. To be efficient, business operations need predictability of clients' behavior, and this means that professionals should promote therapeutic compliance. Adherence to treatment is also, of course, in the best interests of the client, a factor at least as important as business objectives.

If a client is significantly noncompliant with critical policies and procedures, the mental health practitioner should (as in a failure-to-pay case) implement termination and/or referral—again, with care to avoid abandonment. Allowing the client to continue receiving treatment under disadvantageous conditions is hurtful, and continuing to treat someone who is not benefiting may pose an ethical problem (see American Psychological Association, 1981a).

Managing Professionals

Professionals, too, must adhere to policies and procedures, both for clients' welfare and for the business objectives. The mental health CEO presumably will have set up policies and procedures to ensure that an adequate standard of care is inherent in all services provided. Nonadherence by professionals threatens the standard of care, which can lead to poor quality of service to clients and elevate the legal risk for the mental health business.

Since professionals are usually aware of the importance of therapeutic adherence for clients, it would seem that they would have no difficulty adhering to policies and procedures themselves, especially if they have helped shape them and contributed to their development (see Chapter Six). Unfortunately, health-care providers across disciplines may be no better able than clients to adhere to policies and procedures, and they often fail to follow clinical prescriptions and proscriptions (Peterson, Forham, and Jones, 1980; Meichenbaum and Turk, 1987). Even when health-care providers pledge to follow recommended procedures, they adhere to them only a small percentage of the time (McDonald, 1981).

To try to improve adherence among fellow professionals

in the mental health practice, the CEO should explore organizational stressors and factors that undermine motivation to be a team member. Established management incentives, such as rewards, may be useful. The problem, of course, may be more organizational than individual, and systemic revision may be in order. On the individual level, there may be countertransference directed at the organization (for example, rebellion against the authority of the CEO). When this is the reason, it may be helpful to get the nonadhering professional to explain his or her reason for noncompliance, examine how much (if at all) nonadherence is justified by the situation, explore any sources of psychological distortion, and make a self-determined judgment about how to correct feelings, perceptions, beliefs, and behaviors that reflect nonadherence. Of course, if the noncompliant professional is unable or unwilling to engage in this process, the mental health CEO may have to exercise authority by ordering and monitoring adherence or discharging the professional. (Chapter Eight has more to say about the management of professionals through supervision.)

CHAPTER 8

Managing Risks: How to Avoid Ethical, Regulatory, and Legal Complaints

ENTREPRENEURSHIP EMBRACES SEIZING AN OPPORTU-nity—but only after careful calculations of the pluses and minuses. The pluses are the attractive benefits, such as financial gain and personal need fulfillment. The negatives are the un-attractive penalties, such as the risks of failure. The positives cannot be allowed to overshadow the negatives. The quest for positives can be abruptly halted by negatives. This chapter ad-dresses the ominous area of risk management; the focus is on avoiding ethical, regulatory, and legal complaints (for more in-formation, see Woody, 1988a, 1988b).

Defining Risk Management

By definition, risk management has a distinct connection with good business. Risk management is part of the mental health CEO's decisions about the type of business entity to adopt, the kinds and amounts of insurance coverage to purchase, the timing and placement of investments, the marketing plan(s), the management of services and accounts, and the allocation of resources. Clearly, each of these areas has relevance to business success or failure.

In a more clinical framework, risk management encompasses decisions on services to be provided and on staff assignments for clients' care. In other words, a scope of services that cannot be ably covered by the professionals within the particular mental health practice can lead to a risk of inadequate care; consequently, a high standard of care, essential to avoiding negligence, is at risk. A breach of the standard of care, by omission or commission, is the basis for a complaint, and in this era of heightened public concern about good health care, the consequences can have a grave impact on the overall status of the mental health business.

Risk management is concerned with optimal performance, thereby producing business benefits. It is also concerned with proactively protecting the practice from onslaughts from external sources, such as lawsuits by clients. This is honorably accomplished by the development and maintenance of policies and procedures that protect consumers and, in the process, protect the mental health business. There should be no effort to use subterfuge or other dubious tactics to avoid social responsibility; rather, there should be an unrelenting commitment to ethically and legally sound operations and services. Satisfied customers increase the likelihood of repeat or new business and decrease the likelihood of ethical, third-party, regulatory, and legal complaints.

The Nature of Complaints

Society has given the mental health professional a privilege: an opportunity to provide health-care services. This privilege is not to be taken lightly; it is a privilege, not an inalienable right. Through governmental regulation (such as licensing), public policy awards "professionalism" temporarily to those with certain educational, academic, and personal attributes. The award is never permanent. It is renewed only if the professional continues to practice his or her discipline in a manner that benefits the public. If operational or service quality falls, disciplinary options safeguard the public welfare.

Ethical Complaints. In earlier years, society trusted professional disciplines to police their own members. There was much reliance on ethical sanctions, such as when an association's ethics committee intervened in behalf of a client who complained about the poor quality of care. Too often, it seemed to society, these collegial efforts were well intended but ineffective. As mental health care became widely accepted and was considered essential and integral to the social system, mental health practitioners came under closer scrutiny. When they appeared to move toward a business model, the public increasingly questioned the appropriateness of near-exclusive control of standards and discipline by members of professional disciplines. While ethics committees still exist, they currently have far less authority; their control is essentially restricted to allowing practitioners to remain in an association. (In fairness to the ethics committees, however, it must be said that some are now aggressively seeking to inform other bodies, such as state licensing boards, of unethical conduct by members.)

The public demand for accountability, such as through imposing liability for wrongful conduct, has led some professional associations to restructure the scope and functions of ethics committees. According to the American Psychological Association (1987b, p. 730), "at least eight state associations have disbanded their ethics committees and are using those committees solely for educative and referral purposes in order to protect themselves from potential legal liability. This issue is confounded by state associations either having difficulty obtaining liability insurance or not being able to afford adequate coverage. Although individual ethics committee members would be covered by their own policies, the association risks liability with an ethics adjudication program." The move has been to seek ethical review at the national level, which obviously creates problems of resources, immediacy, and logistics. The alternative has been to transfer the function to other disciplinary measures, such as complaints to state regulatory boards and malpractice suits in courts of law.

Third-Party Complaints. Now that so many mental health clients are covered by health insurance, the third-party payer has a definite interest in the quality of care provided to its insured. Granted, the insurance company's interest may be based more on concern about minimizing its own expenditures than on concern about maximizing personal benefits to the client (perhaps the two aims are not, in fact, separable). All the same, the third-party payer's scrutiny furthers the client's interests by subjecting health-care services to quality assurance. It is common for an insurance carrier to require that an approved provider have certain qualifications and to have a member of the professional discipline review case reports (the latter procedure is termed *peer review*). Discipline would probably amount, at the most, to removing the mental health practitioner from the list of approved providers. There have been cases, however, in which the third-party payer has required refunds of money dispensed to mental health practitioners who were discovered not to have met prescribed standards.

Regulatory Complaints. Today, the front-line protector of public welfare is the state regulatory agency. States vary greatly in their rigor and in successful policing by their state regulatory offices: "Through its licensing laws, a state controls the mental health services made available to its citizenry. A state agency, such as a department of professional regulation or a bureau of examining boards (or similar title), is designated to implement the regulatory law. It does so by developing regulations, rules, advisory opinions, or guidelines for defining acceptable and unacceptable acts (again, whether by omission or commission) on the part of the practitioner. In developing and enforcing these regulations, nonprofessionals in the agency may be assisted by a board composed of professionals from the discipline *and* one or more representatives of the public (laypersons placed on the board to symbolize its accountability to the public)" (Woody, 1988b, p. 10). A violation of a state statute relevant to licensing may lead to criminal and administrative action, and disciplinary action may include incarceration, fines, reprimands, and suspension or revocation of one's license. Many state boards have interstate reporting systems, which prevent practitioners who have been disciplined from moving to other states and resuming practice with impunity.

Sometimes a complaint to a state licensing board is a first step toward a civil legal action. For example, a client who has suffered damages due to malpractice by a mental health professional may file a complaint with the state regulatory agency. If the complaint is upheld, it may be a strong predicate for a tort (a civil wrong causing a compensatory injury).

Legal Complaints. It is an understatement to say that today's mental health professional, regardless of his or her qualifications or context, practices in a litigious era and is at high risk for a legal complaint. Legal complaints against mental health professionals are on the rise (Fisher, 1985). Moreover, the availability of malpractice insurance is restricted, and its cost continues to climb (Goodstein, 1986). According to McCarthy (1986, p. 2), "The malpractice issue, whether called a crisis or a breakdown, has four sides: patients, doctors, lawyers, and insurers. With immense sums of money at stake, doctors nearsightedly see lawyers as enemies and patients as potential enemies. That leaves the insurers free to raise malpractice rates to unprecedented heights. Of the three professional groups, the insurers have been making the weakest justifications for their soaring fees." Whatever the source of the malpractice crisis, the facts remain: The threat of legal action is real and must be countered by the mental health CEO, and important assets, including one's professional reputation, are endangered by a legal complaint (see Woody, 1988a, for additional analysis of the malpractice crisis).

A legal complaint must be supported by a reasonable cause of action—that is, any allegation must rest on a legal theory and principles that will justify the involvement of the legal system. As mental health services have gained increased acceptance by society, the legal system has accommodated an increase in the number and types of causes of action. It is beyond the scope of this chapter to detail the legal nature of causes of action, but clarification and a few examples are in order.

After reviewing malpractice cases against psychotherapists, Hogan (1979, p. 18) concluded, "Despite the myriad of actions available, the simple negligence or malpractice suit is by far the most preferred by plaintiffs, occurring in more than half of all cases, and more than five times as frequently as the next common legal action, which is deprivation of one's constitutional rights." Negligence is defined by breach (by omission or commission) of a standard of care. For mental health professionals, this means failing to provide services in a manner consonant with what the reasonable and prudent mental health professional of similar ilk would provide. Negligence requires four elements (Keeton, Dobbs, Keeton, and Owen, 1984). First, there must be a duty or obligation that is recognized by law (for example, a mental health practitioner must protect his or her clients from unreasonable risks). Second, there must be a failure to meet, or a breach of, the standard of care that is applicable to the situation (for example, the practitioner's failure to use adequate professional judgment or skill). Third, the failure or breach must have a causal connection to a resulting injury (for example, a practitioner's intentionally causing mental distress to a client or entering into an inappropriate, perhaps sexual, relationship with a client). Fourth, there must be actual loss or damage that is compensable (for example, a judgment of a certain amount of money for the damage suffered because of the malpractice).

Besides negligence and sexual misconduct or impropriety, other causes of action include incorrect treatment, improper child placement or removal (including faulty testimony in custody disputes), breach of confidentiality, wrongful death of the client or others, malicious infliction of emotional stress, improper administrative handling, violation of civil rights, bodily injury to a client, defamation (libel or slander), failure to supervise a client properly (resulting in injury to the client or others), suicide of a client, failure to make a proper diagnosis, assault and battery (including inappropriate touching), breach of contract, failure to cure, failure to refer, accident on the premises, and undue influence (Besharov, 1985; Hogan, 1979; Trent, 1978). For the plaintiff's attorney, developing a legitimate cause of action can be a stimulating and creative endeavor; mental health services, with their humanistic and ill-defined composition, provide fertile motivational ground.

Effects of a Complaint

The effects that are possible from a complaint are never positive. It is truly a matter of damage control, trying to minimize the negative fallout and avoid the probable devastation to reputation, career, and business.

An untold number of complaints are resolved between the two parties (the mental health practitioner and the disgruntled client), and that is as it should be. The professional should be cautious, however, about attempting a personal resolution; often, it becomes a "foot in the mouth" exercise. If the practitioner retains professional control of the negotiations, the resolution is subject to being set aside later because of the professional's "undue influence" over the client. If the practitioner leaves his or her professional stance and becomes an equal party in an attempt at conflict resolution, there may be a dilution of the professional helping role. For the client, it can be a dismantling of all the accomplishments that may have been obtained throughout treatment. For the professional, it is naked vulnerability, and anything that is said is subject to the client's passing it on to an attorney. When there is a dispute with a client, the mental health practitioner, in this litigious era, may be in a disadvantageous position. If the client's objections and complaints are fueled by pathology, as is often the case, the mental health practitioner should own up to several facts: He or she has lost control of therapeutic communication, there is the specter of legal action, inept handling of a complaint can produce lasting negative results, and it is time to become defensive and seek a supportive alliance with his or her own attorney.

The majority of formal legal actions are settled out of court, but such resolution is seldom if ever without severe negative effects. On the basis of his study of settlement cases, Wright (1981, p. 1538) states, "Although the claim was settled at the nuisance level (less than $5,000), the psychologist experienced considerable personal stress and invested many hours of non-remunerative time." The consequences can affect one's personal health and family life, finances, and career (Charles, Wilbert, and Kennedy, 1984).

Too often, the practitioner believes that the filing of a lawsuit will lead to his or her malpractice insurance carrier's providing an unreserved legal defense, only to discover with dismay that the malpractice insurance policy contains exclusionary language (for example, it excludes coverage for certain kinds of alleged acts, such as sexual misconduct) and restrictions on legal representation. On the latter point, policies typically prescribe that the insurance company will select the attorney. When the insurance company pays the fee, it is understandable that the attorney may tend to pursue objectives that are dominated by the preferences of the insurance carrier, as opposed to those of the practitioner. Moreover, it is common to allow the insurance company to decide when a settlement offer should be accepted. If the practitioner opposes the settlement, perhaps to preserve his or her reputation, he or she may have to hire independent legal counsel.

With respect to finances, there are many expenditures beyond what might be paid for by a malpractice insurance policy. Most notably, a considerable amount of time must be devoted to preparing a legal defense, and this means time away from the office and from generating income. Further, there is reason to believe that the litigant-practitioner commonly experiences debilitating emotions that lessen his or her work productivity and income. Turkington (1986, p. 6) writes, "Even a victory—and 70 percent of the suits against psychologists are settled in their favor—can be crippling. A nuisance suit that never gets to court can cost as much as $50,000 in legal fees." Whatever the source of the money—an insurance carrier or the practitioner—the defense against a legal complaint is expensive. The same is true for the defense against an ethical or regulatory complaint. It should be noted that malpractice insurance seldom covers legal representation from ethical or regulatory complaints, and attorneys' fees must be paid from the practitioner's funds.

If a case goes to trial, a plaintiff's judgment will specify financial damages (see Woody, 1988a, pp. 51–55, for the types of damages). While a judgment may be paid by the malpractice insurance carrier, the judgment may exceed the coverage. Keep in mind that public policy does not provide a corporate shield to protect the mental health CEO from his or her own malpractice, and so personal assets will be at risk.

The mental health entrepreneur knows that money can always be replaced by hard work. What cannot be replaced, and what may be irreparably damaged, is professional status or reputation. If the mental health practitioner has any one most valued asset, it is reputation, which is necessary to gain referrals. Even when a complaint is frivolous and an allegation totally false, there is risk to professional reputation. Certainly, the wish of an insurance company to settle a complaint in order to avoid a buildup of attorneys' fees stands to benefit the carrier but harm the practitioner. Despite their training, mental health professionals are assuredly not above gossip, and an undocumented rumor about a practitioner can circulate unchecked through the community. Even without any verification of a plaintiff's allegations, community sources have been known to shy away from making referrals to a practitioner who was once, perhaps long before, embroiled in a complaint.

Preparing for a Complaint

Unpleasant as it may be, today's mental health CEO must accept the omnipresent risk of complaint. This attitude is not paranoia; it is simply part of the reality of mental health practice. The risk exists regardless of one's mental health discipline, amount of training, years of experience, gender, age, or any other variable. The only solution is to construct and maintain a risk-management system in the mental health organization.

In the service of entrepreneurship, the risk-management system should be conceived of as a guardian of assets, not as a dampener on business innovation or aggressiveness. The costs associated with a risk-management system (such as paying an attorney for legal information and for opinions on day-to-day operations) should be thought of as reasonable and necessary expenses of doing business. A practitioner would not dream of providing services without an office, a desk, and so on, and should entertain no fantasies of being able to make legally oriented decisions, especially about case management, without the advice of counsel.

Compliance with risk-management policies and procedures should be required of clients, associated professionals, and support staff members (see Chapter Seven). Anyone who cannot or will not adhere to risk-management conditions should be viewed as an unacceptable threat to the mental health organization and should receive outplacement counseling. After reasonable educative and shaping efforts, noncompliant clients should be properly terminated and/or referred, and associated professionals and support staff members should be dismissed from employment.

Risk-Management Strategies

Earlier chapters have presented numerous ideas about structuring the mental health business to minimize and control risks. Knowledgeably selecting professional affiliates and the business entity (Chapter Five), carefully managing human resources (Chapter Six) and operations (Chapter Seven), and conducting thoughtful business planning (Chapter Two)—all lead to market success and to conditions that will accommodate effective risk management. There are, however, three strategies that should be adopted.

Strategy One: Maintain Prudent Self-Regulation. Within the mental health organization, all professional associates and support staff members must be dedicated to prudent conduct—every thought and action must be reasonable and based on academic and professional standards. It is unlikely that this goal will be fulfilled through authoritarian dictates; self-regulation will be required. Consequently, the mental health CEO should promote policies that will reward colleagues and employees for this sort of self-governed compliance, in the interest of risk management for the mental health organization.

A fundamental of self-regulation for risk management is to avoid any suggestion of competence that is not factual and well documented. No position or title should be conferred or accepted without supportive reason, nor should vanity ever lead to quasi-professional representations or connections with self-aggrandizing professional conglomerates (for example, groups that readily bestow certificates on members—for a fee, of course). Rather, one's allegiance should be to understatement (relying on only the most unimpeachable qualifications) and one's affiliation should be limited to standards-setting professional associations. No claim of special expertise should ever be made or accepted without solid proof of competence from a recognized authority.

Personal integrity is indispensable to risk management. Along with malpractice insurance, having a supervisory relationship—especially with an objective, high-status professional source—is one of the best ways to minimize the risk of a complaint. There can be no overreliance on independent judgment, such as about how to best treat a client. Mental health CEOs should make provisions for close supervision of everyone in their organizations, including themselves. The emphasis here is on personal receptivity to having one's professional activities monitored by a supervisor. As part of the commitment to good health care required by public policy, the mental health professional is obligated to seek help that will ensure his or her clients' best interests, whether through supervision or continuing education.

The practitioner must accept that mental health services fall within the business arena. This attitude is essential to risk management. If today's mental health practitioner attempts to treat clients and emphasize only certain humanistic conditions (as was done in public policy in the 1960s), risk will be high. Nowadays, there must be hard-nosed pragmatism, with objective, academically supported, change-oriented methods. Today's practitioner needs to be aware of current developments in therapy, techniques, and accountability and incorporate this awareness into standards for client care.

Strategy Two: Control Professional Associates and Support Staff Members. Repeated comments have been made about the need to be highly selective about persons associated with the mental health practice. This recommendation is for both business and risk-management reasons: The "master-servant" or *Respondeat Superior* principles can foster vicarious liability, especially for anyone with a supervisory role. Certainly, the mental health CEO is at risk for the conduct, by omission or commission, of every employee, whether a professional or a support staff member, in the organization. Consequently, full disclosure of all prospective employees' professional and personal qualities should be a condition of employment with the mental health practice. Even then, continued close supervision, regardless of staff members' seniority, should be maintained.

If there is a transgression of a policy or a procedure, a written objection should be issued, and corrective steps (based on the advice of legal counsel) should be taken immediately. Defensiveness can be healthy, and an attorney can be an important ally.

Strategy Three: Adopt Legally Safe Policies and Procedures. A crucial method for avoiding faults is to have policies and procedures that ensure a clear understanding of what is expected. Among many other possibilities, this means having detailed job descriptions, comprehensive (written) policies and procedures, and contracts about liability. The latter would detail any insurance coverage and could contain provisions for indemnification, whereby whoever was responsible for the legally related expense would have to reimburse those who incurred expense through vicarious liability.

The mental health practice should predicate its services on providing all clients and their significant others with information about what can be expected within the service framework. The earlier discussion on promotional strategies (Chapter Four) described the contents of a service brochure, which is an excellent way of providing clients with information for risk-management purposes. Among other important risk-management issues, the financial policies should be well known and debts by clients should be avoided.

The policies and procedures should be in accord with the particular ethics applicable to the professionals associated with the mental health practice. Few if any conflicts exist among the various sets of ethics endorsed by the primary mental health professional associations, but certain disciplines do have unique specifics. Given his or her responsibility for leadership, the mental health CEO should be well versed in each of the relevant codes of ethics. Moreover, certain disciplines are promulgating standards for service delivery (for example, American Psychological Association, 1981b, 1987a). This type of position statement on standards is especially crucial to risk management and would probably be almost determinative in establishing the standard of care in an ethical, regulatory, or legal hearing. Consequently, the management of operations should enforce the prescriptions and proscriptions contained in the ethical and service-delivery materials of the relevant disciplines. Of course, there may be certain parochial considerations—for example, community standards in southern California might be quite different from those in Alabama.

Having laid a legally safe foundation through the selection of a business entity for the mental health practice, one supports the organizational structure by a proper standard of care. The standard of care is embodied in policies and procedures, which are made known to clients, associated professionals, and support staff members. Adherence to the standard of care is a necessary defense against allegations of negligence. Therefore, the standard of care should be derived from professional ethics and service-delivery guidelines and implemented with recognition of the strengths and weaknesses unique to the mental health practice and its resources. In other words, inappropriately broad or superficial services should be avoided in favor of a restrictive scope of service that will be sure to meet the prevailing standard of care. (Of course, the scope of services must also reflect the marketing objectives.) To prevent misunderstandings, the standard of care should be formed with the help of the associated professionals and support staff members, and it should be explained to all clients (and their significant others) with full disclosure (so as to provide a legal defense). There should be no "puffing" that might lead clients to reasonably expect certain qualifications or results that are not part of the true standard of care, and there should certainly be no semblance of any guaranteed outcome of treatment. The mental health practitioner's occasional duty to breach confidentiality and privileged communications (as, perhaps, in being required to report certain kinds of abuse and to warn of a client's dangerousness) should be made clear to the client from the first meeting.

Records (see Chapter Seven) can be the basis of essential defensive information and evidence. For example, documenting disclosures to clients and quality of treatment is necessary for risk management. Similarly, having clients review and approve all communications may be a challenge at times, but it can help one avoid allegations of slander, libel, or unauthorized release of information. Care should be taken to be sure that records contain complete information on what the professional and the clients said and did during interventions.

Most important, clinical procedures must be controlled by prudence and well-established theories and practices. Innovation is possible, but it must be used wisely and subjected to peer review or supervision, to ensure that the best interests of the client are safeguarded. In keeping with certain ethical notions, clients should be informed (and this act should be documented) of one's reservations about the effectiveness of innovations. There should be an individual treatment plan, based on acceptable diagnostic data, and the client should provide informed consent and acknowledge having received information on any possible negative effects. There should be special policies and procedures to deal with dangerousness, emergencies, termination, and follow-up. The principal guideline is that reasonable expertise must be used, and the client should not be unreasonably subjected to the possibility of harm due to the practitioner's judgment. A business purpose might be served by termination of certain clients, for example, but abrupt termination that risks abandonment is unacceptable. For risk management, it should be a standard procedure to follow up with every former client and check on how he or she is doing after treatment, and the follow-up contact should be entered in the client's record. Established referral and emergency sources are also useful.

One's professionalism is always influenced by one's personal qualities, and so policies and procedures should safeguard against moments of personal weakness. Affiliation with the mental health practice group should require an appropriate lifestyle. While this dictate can create a clash between business interests and individual rights, the focus here is on entrepreneurship and successful business; philosophical debates can be conducted elsewhere. From the standpoint of entrepreneurship and business objectives, personal conduct must not detract from professional standards and business goals. Thus, personal qualities and opinions should pass through a "better business" filter. Perhaps above all else, this means that the practitioner should have no contact with any client (or any significant other) that is not in the unilateral best interests of the client. Given the complexities of couple and family therapy, it is often unclear who the client is, and nebulous ethical principles create risk for the practitioner. If risk management is to be effective, contacts with clients must be strictly professional and strictly for business.

CHAPTER 9

Leadership in Your Mental Health Practice

THE MENTAL HEALTH PROFESSIONAL'S PHILOSOPHI-cal framework can constrict leadership and, as a result, the effectiveness of the practice. As mentioned in Chapter One, the mental health professional may be prone to believe that every professional associated with the practice should be equal. This belief can hamper entrepreneurial efforts. In fact, every associated practitioner will not be equal, whether he or she is measured by clinical skills, operational efficiency, or contribution to developing the practice. A basic premise of successful business is that each practitioner's rights, authority, and benefits derive from his or her contribution to production. There can be no preordained status; it must be earned.

Theories of Leadership

Lewin, Lippett, and White (1939) established conclusively that, among autocratic, democratic, and laissez-faire types of leadership, democratic leadership engenders the greatest group cohesion and task fulfillment. (There is, of course, much more to the makeup of leadership than simply one of these labels.)

There are varied beliefs about what produces leadership. The "great person" theory holds that certain people have unique traits, and their exceptionality guarantees leadership. Analysis of studies of the personal factors associated with leadership reveal myriad traits—physique, fluency of speech, intelligence, scholarship, originality, adaptability, dominance, responsibility, and prestige, to name but a few (Stogdill, 1948; Worchel and Cooper, 1983).

The Backdrop of Leadership

It could be argued that every mental health professional, by virtue of having attained advanced academic credentials, has established a potential for leadership. For our purposes here, that premise can be accepted, but with the obvious caveat that the potential for many will not be realized. Therefore, we will focus on how the mental health entrepreneur can assess his or her capacity and implement means of fulfilling the personal potential for leadership.

Before we move ahead, however, we should recognize several conditions. First, a mental health practice represents an organization. No matter how many practitioners are involved, this is still true. Even a practice consisting of a solo practitioner with a minimal support staff (such as a spouse who helps with nitty-gritty tasks) is an organization. Second, a mental health organization consists of a system, a complex set of interacting factors. Third, a successful mental health practice requires leadership. (Incidentally, while the foregoing does apply to the solo practitioner, entrepreneurship requires the timely addition of personnel, and most mental health practices will involve an array of human resources.) In support of both the progress of health care as a business and the surge in entrepreneurship, Parsons, Youkstetter, Burton, and Willson (1986) report an increase in group practices.

With this organizational-systemic-leadership backdrop, the mental health professional accepts the reins for controlling the team: "Leaders are the cultural guardians of organizations. They create and maintain the attitudes, habits, beliefs and traditions that make each organization unique. By focusing on the qualitative side, leaders can begin to create cultural fabrics that bind people together, that motivate people in the setting, and that provide people with a sense of belonging and continuity"

(Boje and Ulrich, 1985, pp. 312–313). Clearly, the leader's skills must complement the organizational-systemic components, such as through uniting people for effectiveness and productivity.

The Role of the CEO

The mental health CEO is responsible for every aspect of the practice. There can be no shirking of responsibility. For example, one CEO contacted me for legal counsel about a problem created by one of his associates, saying, "Of course, he caused it, so if there is a legal problem, it's his, not mine." Aside from his ignorance of vicarious liability, this professional, notwithstanding his senior status in the practice, was revealing that he was unable to accept responsibility for the operations: He did not truly deserve to be the CEO. The mental health CEO is obliged to own any outcome, be it success or failure. Of course, an associate may have triggered a problem, but the CEO should have been able to activate a safety mechanism to avoid an explosion. Conversely, the wise CEO will welcome an associate's taking pride in a success, knowing that the associate's accomplishment also attests to the CEO's acumen.

Having a Systemic View. The mental health CEO will view the practice as a social system. This means that behavior among the system's members is motivated by individual as well as collective interests and that interdependent processes proceed from the specialization and division of labor (Ruekert and Walker, 1987, p. 2). In other words, what one person does affects or serves as a precondition for what another person does, and the organization operates according to functionally interdependent skills, resources, and capabilities. Thus, when an effort is made to change the operations (perhaps by exercising leadership or implementing a new procedure, such as marketing), it is necessary to analyze all bits of the systemic matrix.

Getting the Job Done. The effective mental health CEO must be a true executive. By definition, the term *executive* connotes "execution" (to put into effect, to carry out, to perform), and there are at least four essential skills:

1. *Interacting.* Managers who have (a) the ability to understand how others feel, and (b) have good bargaining skills, are often the best implementers. Interaction with people inside and outside the corporation is a necessity when new programs, strategies, and tactics are desired.

2. *Allocating.* This activity requires that people and dollars must be allocated among the marketing activities where they will be most effective.

3. *Monitoring.* Successful implementation requires that managers identify the information they need to make good decisions and then utilize the information and control systems to supply that information.

4. *Organizing.* Good execution of marketing tasks requires an ability to match each problem with a particular structure and to change the informal organization to provide such a structure [Hartley and Lee, 1986, p. 29].

The mental health CEO gets the job done. Without competence in execution, none of the strategies offered for business analysis and planning, marketing, and operations management will be effective.

"Making Rain." The mental health CEO must be capable of producing or getting others to produce business. In the business world, garnering new accounts or bringing in business is known as "making rain," and it is essential to entrepreneurship and leadership: "Managing executives and senior partners in professional service firms have at least one thing in common. They all agree that a major criterion for promotion to executive or partnership status is the ability to generate new business. The name given to these all too rare new business developers is revealing— 'Rainmakers.' Rainmakers make things happen" (Wheatley,

1987, p. 73). To earn his or her place in a mental health practice, every professional must be capable of "making rain." People will have varying degrees of success in and responsibility for gaining new business, but it should be a component of every job description in the mental health organization. It is unwise to rely solely or even primarily on the promotional or sales skills of one individual, such as the CEO.

Using Power. Historically, leadership has been aligned with control of power. Power reflects the capacity or potential to influence others and to resist influence from others. The mental health CEO has various types of power, with some being more useful (depending on the circumstances) than others. Power can come from different sources. *Coercive power* relies on potential threats and punishments to force change in behavior. It has many negative features and requires consistent surveillance. *Reward power* uses positive reinforcement and motivates a low-powered person to stay in the relationship, but it is costly and uses up valuable resources. *Legitimate power* is authority in a particular domain. *Expert power* is gained through others' recognition of one's superior knowledge about a particular topic. *Referent power* is fed by admiration. It is very usable, requires no surveillance, and leads to internalization of attitudes (as opposed to mere behavioral conformity). *Informational power* comes from actual knowledge (recognition from others is not necessary) (Worchel and Cooper, 1983).

In a mental health practice, a CEO can use coercive power, but threats and punishment will probably accomplish little or nothing constructive with professional associates. The resources may be controlled by the CEO, but the professional associate has other options and soon rebels against or escapes from coercive conditions. The CEO has definite reward power, whether as income or as eventual partial ownership of the practice. Legitimate power, such as for decisions and behavior to further the operations, is vested with the CEO by designation (title). The CEO's expert power may be mitigated by the fact that associates are also professionals. Expert power and informational power may combine when the CEO purposefully seeks special competence and unique knowledge of material that will not be readily available to others in the practice, such as information on achieving better marketing connections (say, new referral sources) that can increase an associate's caseload and income.

The mental health CEO will apply power to the elements of leadership: the *situation* (task and resources, social structure and rules, physical setting, point in history), the *followers* (expectations, personality characteristics, competence, motivation), and his or her *leadership* factors (legitimacy, competence, motivation, personality characteristics, definition of the situation) (Hollander, 1978). With this analysis, the CEO will formulate a *leadership style.*

Past and Present Styles

The evolution of business leadership style is ever changing and is a function of the setting (mental health practice) and the era (the contemporary positioning of mental health services in society). Ficker (1975) has analyzed the differences between traditional and contemporary, or emerging, leadership styles. He indicates that leadership traditionally went to the power position, authority was delegated without a sharing of responsibility, employees' security came from a guardian-type supervisor, loyalty to the supervisor unified the employees, competition was used to increase production, and the supervisor retained the responsibility for evaluation.

Now leadership is different. The emerging and preferred style allows leadership to other than status positions, shared responsibility and authority with (potentially) the entire work team, involvement in decision making (which provides a sense of security), and group responsibility for employees' evaluation. This style leads employees to achieve unity through consensus and group loyalty, with the highest production occurring in a threat-free climate. This modern conceptualization is compatible with the findings of research in group dynamics (Zander, 1985).

The Heroic Stance Versus the Developmental Stance

It should be apparent that any idea that the CEO must be a hero or a heroine finds no support in current leadership concepts. The CEO is not the sole savior of the organization. No matter how competent, the CEO cannot know what is going on at all times, may not have any more expertise than an associate, and does not guarantee a perfect solution to every problem.

Research does support leadership that is committed to group dynamics and human resource development. Bradford and Cohen (1984) favor a "Manager-as-Developer" model, which is filled with paradoxes: "The Manager-as-Developer has to be both less active and more active than the heroic manager" (p. 283); "The Manager-as-Developer must give greater autonomy to subordinates while establishing more controls" (p. 285); "Manager-as-Developers increase their own power by giving subordinates greater power" (p. 285); "The Manager-as-Developer builds a team as a way to support member individuality" (p. 286); "The Manager-as-Developer model requires an optimistic faith in subordinate possibilities but tough implementation to work" (p. 286); and "Although the Developer model requires new behavior, the best way to improve performance as a manager is to focus on the needs of others, rather than on yourself" (p. 288).

In contrast to the do-it-all-yourself nature of the heroic stance, the developmental stance requires a shared-responsibility team. With this team approach, each person knows what to do, performs tasks well, trusts colleagues, avoids blaming, has latitude for individual decision making (at least in certain areas), accepts that issues must be dealt with by the group, feels no automatic oppositional tendency (but will debate constructively), promotes a supportive organizational climate, seeks to enhance learning and competence for self and others, and facilitates individual and group self-correcting mechanisms (Bradford and Cohen, 1984).

These developmental principles are especially apt for a group of mental health professionals. After all, the mental health group is composed of very bright and well-trained professionals who are inclined to independent thinking and achievement and, above all, are specialists in human behavior. The CEO still wields power (such as by persuasion) and is the ultimate decision maker, but each member feels like an important contributing part of the organization. To try to conduct such an ensemble of professionals from other than a shared-responsibility score would surely lead to dissonance and cacophony. At the same time, the CEO need not relinquish the director's baton.

Being a Great Communicator

The CEO can be short on certain kinds of competence, as long as he or she can communicate effectively. Communication can be internal or external. When marketing is discussed, it will be emphasized that internal communications are essential to successful marketing that is, ostensibly, directed toward external sources; that is, the members of the mental health team are a filter for what others beyond the practice should and will receive. If team members do not understand, accept, and advocate the message, it will fall on deaf ears in the marketplace.

Internal and external communications must convey a sense of authority and certainty, and "given the requisite professional competence and technical knowledge, the professional builds his practice by attracting prospective clients through appropriate visibility techniques, by acquiring an understanding of their needs or problems, and by personally convincing them of his ability to solve them. But the effectiveness of all of these ultimately depend on the individual professional's ability to inspire or to communicate confidence . . . . This is the key to selling professional services, whether one is an individual practitioner or part of a large firm" (Mahon, 1978, p. 16).

Communicating a message of confidence serves to motivate staff members toward high-quality performance, referral sources to respect the competence of the practitioners, and potential and existing clients to trust that they will be well served by the practice. The mental health CEO, therefore, is in control of persuasion to produce a perception of confidence.

Communication by mental health professionals is commonly plagued by "psychojargon" or "psychobabble." Mental health services rely on words that are often tinged with or reflective of pathology. Many people outside (for example, potential clients) not only may be unable to understand such language but may also react defensively against it (and, in the case of clients, avoid the service).

Often a potential client has a preconceived belief about mental health professionals. Whether justified or not, this belief colors perception of the professional's message. In fact, mental health professionals often have the same sorts of biases or prejudices. For example, a professional in one mental health discipline may stereotype a colleague from a different mental health discipline. One practitioner said, "We know social workers are more in tune with feelings than psychologists."

The mental health CEO may wish to capitalize on preconceived notions by poking gentle fun at them, perhaps by introducing himself or herself to a lay audience as a "headshrinker" but then going on to establish respect by taking a scientist-practitioner stance. The mental health CEO must definitely avoid inept use of terms that may be meaningless, frightening, or evoke defensiveness. Word choice must be tailored to the receiver, whether another professional or a layperson.

In communicating with an internal or an external audience, the communicator must be believable, and the message must be relevant to the needs of and comprehensible to the receiver. Delivery must be focused on a purpose, targeted to an audience (or receiver), and paced to the capacity of the receiver-translator. Perhaps above all else, the communication must reflect a sincere respect for the rights and dignity of the receiver.

The communication mettle of the mental health professional is tested in crisis management. Few practices have any communication plan for handling bad press. For example, one practitioner was dismayed when the press reported the suicide of one of his clients. A psychiatric outpatient facility received extensive press coverage about the way it provided for suicidal patients (there was a rash of suicides among its clientele). One female practitioner was reported in the press to have an illicit relationship with a man engaged in a messy custody battle. In each of these instances, a well-planned crisis-management communication strategy was needed: "The first two days of a crisis are the most important because first impressions by the press make for lasting impressions about the organization or individual. Most organizations commit the first deadly sin—by remaining quiet and from this silence the organization might become guilty until proven innocent" (Winston, 1986a, pp. 8–9).

From a legal perspective, there is often a reason for withholding comment until the opportune time (although Winston's basic idea is sound): Through its CEO, the mental health practice should be prepared to implement responsive communication when a crisis occurs. A crisis can have a severe impact on the marketing program (a topic discussed in Chapter Three). For leadership purposes, it is enough to say that the CEO must spearhead planning and communication in the crisis-management strategy; business success may depend on it.

Being a Super Salesperson

If there is any one marketing notion that is repulsive to a mental health professional, it is the idea of selling professional services. Selling is part of marketing, but it also has strong implications for management and must involve a professional. As Mahon (1978, p. 12) describes it, "ultimately it is the professional himself who must make contact with the prospect, hear out his problems, and convince him of his firm's capacity to solve them. His ability to sell derives more from his technical knowledge and experience than from his knowledge of selling and communications. But he cannot relegate the selling task to salesmen or other laymen—for the important element of client confidence would be missing .... Such confidence can be communicated or inspired only by the professional himself."

Distasteful as the image of "super salesperson" may be, it is required in contemporary mental health practice and must be ongoing to retain even an established client's support and acceptance. Mahon (1978, p. 350) says, "To maintain this almost religious fervor, clients must be continuously 'sold.' It is not enough to sell them only once—when they were acquired. The selling effort must persist during the entire association with the client."

Sales are crucial to the marketing program (see Chapter Three). The role of the mental health CEO includes responsibility for maintaining the sales dimension of the organization. To fulfill this objective, the selection of employees, whether other professionals or support staff members, should include an assessment of how well each will facilitate the selling mission. Certain employees may be more involved with selling than others, but all are crucial to success.

Managing the Product

Just as the idea of selling may be repugnant to some practitioners, there may also be resistance to conceptualizing the mental health service as a product. Today's business world accepts that an intangible professional service is in many ways equivalent to a tangible product (there are, of course, differences, and these and other related issues were discussed in Chapter Three). The mental health CEO must manage according to a product orientation, even if the product is a professional service. According to Clewett and Stasch (1974, p. 23), "The product manager's job is to serve as the focal point for planning and coordinating all of the activities required for the growth and profitability of his product. This does not mean that he does all the planning of his product, but it does mean that he sees that all the activities affecting his product are properly planned . . . . he does have the unqualified responsibility for seeing that everything related to his product gets done well and on time." This duty to get the job done rests with the CEO. It requires considerable skill to deal with varied sources and problems. As Clewett and Stasch (1974, p. 23) add, "To carry out this role effectively, he [the CEO] must be able to work with experts on all matters relating to his product, both inside and outside the company. He must be able to rely on his broad product and marketing knowledge, management skills, and sheer persuasiveness to get things planned and accomplished."

The emphasis here is on both internal and external management. Chapters Three and Four focused on external product or professional service management in a marketing framework. It is equally important for the internal management to ensure that the professional service has the support of the employees and is produced with optimum quality and quantity.

Bloom (1976) indicates five important components of being an effective product manager. First, the CEO should be skilled in gathering timely and relevant information, such as about the production and performance of the service, about how competitors perceive and respond to the service, about consumers' attitudes and habits, and about pertinent governmental regulations. Second, the CEO should be adept at planning marketing strategies, using both short- and long-range marketing plans. Third, the CEO should make reasonably accurate forecasts or predictions of the market's receptivity to the service (the salability of the professional service). Fourth, the CEO should be proficient at coordinating persons and processes. Fifth, the CEO should monitor the progress of the marketing program for the service, quickly identifying if or when there is nonadherence to the marketing plan and implementing remedial changes aimed at ensuring success.

Managing Time

The makeup of the CEO's duties places a premium on time. The CEO must be action-oriented, which means getting problems solved and tasks completed quickly and according to a demanding schedule. Success in business rests on timely performance and efficiency. The executive's ability to perform and execute operations, his or her personal health and life, the organization's success—all hinge on proper and constructive use of time.

Notwithstanding their profound knowledge of human behavior and health, many mental health professionals are prone to abuse themselves and their families through improper use of time. Those in private practice (as opposed to those who are on a salary) are especially vulnerable. Private practitioners often reason that they must never restrict the hours devoted to clients, because to do so would mean losing money. In fact, however, unless the hours devoted to client contact or other work-related activity are reasonably restricted and controlled, professional and personal failure may follow. In the long run, workaholism will lead to the sacrifice of personal happiness (such as through inadequate time with family members) and recreation, as well as to the loss of health (such as through stress).

Personnel are a major investment of the mental health practice; business potential will never be fully realized with faulty personnel. It is part of the CEO's role to promote the mental and physical health of everyone in the practice. The mental health CEO must be sure that the management system places high priority on the efficient and healthful use of time; "despite a certain heroic aura borne by the 84-hour week, it is really dysfunctional and can almost always be shown to be due to poor planning, rather than heroic devotion" (Baty, 1981, p. 182).

After ten hours of work, efficiency tapers off rapidly, to the point where it may take four hours to accomplish what could earlier have been accomplished in one. A too-demanding schedule, even if voluntarily maintained by the CEO, gives a tacit message to other employees that will strain relations and be counterproductive. Baty (1981) recommends the following guidelines.

1. Identify each person's "creativity cycle" and schedule accordingly.
2. Limit a day's schedule to specific and attainable goals.
3. Avoid interruptions (ignore the telephone).
4. Save some time (at the less creative point of the day) to work outside the office (perhaps on special projects).
5. Batch necessary interruptions (have a particular time for unscheduled, walk-in discussions).
6. Group travel commitments.
7. Do all correspondence at one time.
8. Use electronic technology to save time.
9. Set aside time for rumination or thinking.

10. Avoid situations that require unnecessarily prompt responses, since these can lead to overload.
11. Exercise regularly.
12. Get out of the office for revitalization.
13. Employ the principle of "enlightened procrastination" (many problems go away if they are ignored).

These guidelines can be used by the CEO or by employees, their specific relevance depending on the individual's job and role.

It is also wise to have a written schedule. Recall that "work expands to fill the time available." Schedule planning should employ an estimated time allotment and a log for when a task is started and finished. It is helpful to accommodate personal preferences, as long as the task is completed properly. For example, the mental health professional may do a much better job of dictating diagnostic reports or case notes at home than at the office. In urban areas, allowing an employee to save commuting time by working at home may well increase production. Special demands (meeting a deadline or working overtime) or accomplishments (bringing in new business, volunteering to give a speech to a community group, getting a scholarly article published) should be rewarded with a bonus, such as paid time off or a gift. Similarly, special support from an employee's family (a spouse's attending a meeting to further the social attractiveness of the practice) should be recognized (a word of thanks or praise is important) and rewarded (perhaps by a gift). Time must be managed to maximize energy, motivation, health, and productivity, and the bulk of the load rests on the shoulders of the CEO.

The Successful CEO

Success must be individually defined. One professional may define it primarily by annual income; another may define it by a sense of satisfaction. It would be presumptuous to assert that there is only one kind of successful mental health CEO. At the same time, it is important to raise the question of what constitutes success in mental health practice. Some CEOs may seem successful, but close inspection often reveals professional limitations (inadequate training, poor clinical skills) or character flaws (alcoholism, substance abuse, smoking, obesity, sex addiction, inability to love, or whatever). When we consider the tenets of entrepreneurship, two CEO prototypes emerge. The following two prototypes are free of notable deficits and reflect accomplishments that most mental health professionals would respect and possibly relish.

CEO I and CEO II received their graduate degrees from comparable university training programs. They entered private clinical practice in the same year, are about the same age, live in the same community, and have impeccable professional credentials. Each is committed to ethics and to a high standard of care and is recognized for a scholarly approach to practice (although neither writes for publication), honesty, friendliness, communication skills, cautiousness (about legal liability), respect for colleagues and employees, benevolence, a conservative life-style, and devotion to family. While physically healthy, both tend to be a bit overweight. Both rarely drink alcohol. Neither one smokes or would consider substance abuse. Both place business uppermost in their lives, work ten or more hours per day, seven days per week, and take several short family vacations each year. Both rely heavily on their spouses (each works full-time in the respective practice), attorneys, and accountants for business advice, and each has one professional associate and two secretaries. So much for the similarities; now for the differences.

The CEO I Prototype

Work Style. CEO I gets to the office early (seldom after 7:00 A.M.). This person also leaves work early (usually before 5:00 P.M.), which allows time to be with his or her children after school. CEO I works and communicates rapidly and efficiently. For example, any written communication to a potential client is followed up with a personal telephone call. Needing to expand and wishing to upgrade the workplace, CEO I periodically moves to larger and better office space, and plans soon to buy a building. Any advance in high technology is adopted quickly (computerization of accounts and test scoring, high-speed photo-copier, and so on), and CEO I pays for any training needed by employees (CEO I, also, is well versed in computers). This CEO's reading centers on professional material that has practical ideas. He or she is open to new ideas, such as about how to improve marketing.

Marketing Stance. If necessary, CEO I will make an immediate trip anywhere in the country to gain a new referral source, with first-class trappings for client development. This person emphasizes communication strategies with referral sources but generously wines and dines them as well. He or she is active in community affairs, entering each new relationship with consideration for how it can bring new business to the practice. CEO I advertises his or her professional services nationally.

Investment Stance. CEO I is constantly searching for new business avenues, saying, "I'll take a risk on any sound investment." After a careful analysis, this person will readily put money on the line to make it work. If a promotional project fails, he or she will analyze and learn from the situation and say to advisers, with no remorse, "What do we try next?"

Life-Style. CEO I lives in a house valued at about $500,000, has substantial retirement and investment plans, and has no debts to speak of (having paid cash for a major addition to the house). When CEO I gets home at night, he or she puts work out of mind, and gives unreserved attention to family and friends. At home, CEO I has exercise equipment and a swimming pool and regularly uses them. He or she enjoys spectator and participation sports to a modest degree. Family vacations tend to be "far from the madding crowd." This person attends professional conferences and enjoys continuing education but considers it a work situation, not a vacation.

Self-Assessment of Success. Over the past five years, CEO I's gross income has more than doubled each year; taxable income amounted to about $500,000 in 1988. When asked if he or she is happy, CEO I quickly says, "I sure am, but I want to do better!" When asked about goals, this person responds, "To keep the business growing, and to spend more time with my spouse and kids."

The CEO II Prototype

Work Style. CEO II gets to the office about 9:00 A.M., preferring to sleep as late as possible. This person stays at the office until evening (typically until about 7:00 P.M.). He or she works methodically and communicates slowly, weighing every nuance. CEO II's office has been in the same building since the practice was opened. Office equipment consists of one electric typewriter and an inexpensive copier (which operates slowly and requires frequent repair). Also, after many months of contemplation, CEO II purchased a microcomputer. Rather than pay for computer training for his or her longtime secretary, CEO II insisted that the secretary study a book at home, and consequently her competence is limited. CEO II knows little about the computer but is delighted with its ability to score tests. He or she is proud of being well read, and will spend hours at home alone with a book. He or she particularly enjoys material that provides theoretical ideas.

Marketing Stance. CEO II does not seek new business but says with pleasure, "I've been in town so long, people know that I'm here, and I can just sit back and the referrals will come in—my referral sources are going to stick with me." This person does not participate in community affairs. His or her only advertisement is a two-inch listing in the yellow pages of the telephone directory.

Investment Stance. When discussing possible new projects or services, CEO II enters readily into a scholarly analysis of their strengths and weaknesses but inevitably concludes, "It sounds like a good idea, but I don't want to take on anything new. I would rather do what I do at a better level of quality." Unapologetically, he or she says, "I'm just not willing to risk what I've got going for me, no matter how solid the idea."

Life-Style. CEO II lives in a house valued at about $150,000 and has small retirement and investment plans. He or she has a number of debts (including a second home mortgage). This person puts off buying new things until he or she is sure of being able to make the payments. When CEO II gets home at night, he or she is generally tired and seldom goes out except to take the family to a restaurant. CEO II engages in no activity or recreation except for reading professional books and journals. Family vacations tend to be at the hotel where a professional mental health conference is being held (CEO II enjoys continuing education).

Self-Assessment of Success. Over the past five years, CEO II's gross income has increased about 10 percent each year, with his or her taxable income being about $50,000 in 1988. When asked if he or she is happy, CEO II ponders the question and says, "Yes, I like things the way they are now." When asked about goals, he or she contemplates the apparent options and responds, "Just to keep on working, maybe seeing fewer clients in the years to come."

Comparative Analysis of the Two Prototypes

In comparing CEO I and CEO II, it is tempting to explain their differences as reflections of their personalities, priorities, values, and needs, or simply of chance. That is an inadequate explanation. In fact, there are few significant differences in those areas, although over the years the differences in professional style have led to varying emphases relevant to personalities, priorities, values, and needs; but chance has figured in very little.

As a person, each deserves recognition for his or her personal, family, and social values and morals. As a practitioner, each has earned respect. As a CEO, each has performed admirably. In other words, CEO I and CEO II are honorable and successful; neither can justly be denigrated. Their success certainly cannot be measured solely by their incomes or their life-styles.

CEO I can be distinguished by his or her allegiance to and pursuit of entrepreneurship. For the most part, this person personifies the successful entrepreneur. He or she seeks new and practical ideas, is action- and change-oriented, communicates superbly, operates efficiently and according to a business plan, follows a marketing scheme, engages in moderate or calculated risk taking, invests in both the present and the future, manages personnel and other resources wisely, and keeps personal and familial well-being sacrosanct.

CEO II does not embrace entrepreneurship. This person likes new information but does not translate it into action or change. CEO II's communications are adequate but cautiously restricted. He or she moves ahead rather methodically, seldom venturing from the established pathway. Marketing is important only to maintain the status quo. He or she appreciates but does not invest in personnel or other resources. CEO II finds it difficult to keep business from interfering with personal and familial well-being.

Between the CEO I and CEO II prototypes, there are of course gradations of various factors. The challenge to the mental health CEO is to choose a basic prototype, determine what is required to attain it, decide whether he or she has the wherewithal to bring it about, and then live happily with the decision.

CHAPTER 10

Integrating Professional
and Personal Roles
for Business Success

UP TO THIS POINT, THIS BOOK HAS FOCUSED ON HOW
public policy has moved the mental health professions from a
social service model to a health-care business model: the theoretical principles of business and marketing; practical strategies
for creating business and marketing plans, along with promotional ideas; guidance for considering a solo or independent
practice versus a group practice; information about the dynamics unique to a mental health practice group; ways to manage
operations and risk; and leadership in mental health business
efforts. In each of these areas, the mental health practitioner's
personal qualities and life are relevant: They influence health-
care business actions and are, in return, influenced by business
encounters. Business success is integral to personal health and
happiness, and vice versa. Therefore, it is only proper for this
concluding chapter to consider the integration of the practitioner's professional and personal self-concepts.

No matter what one's professional competence or personal characteristics, the effective and healthy blending of the
professional and personal self-concepts will be a constant challenge throughout one's career. The challenge will not be satisfied by mere stability of income; it requires a continual press
toward more enriched self-understanding.

Entrepreneurship and Professional and Personal Priorities

A first step toward integrating the professional and personal self-concepts is to accept that entrepreneurship and professionalism are not, under today's public policy, antithetical. Professional ethics cannot justly denounce a professional self-concept that embraces entrepreneurship, and the therapeutic alliance no longer requires denial of the practitioner's entitlement to benefits beyond altruistic rewards.

This book has illustrated that entrepreneurship involves more than large profits or a large number of clients. Entrepreneurship relies on fulfillment of all sorts of personal and social needs. To be sure, some of these needs may be career-oriented, but others are highly personal—that is, entrepreneurship can provide benefits for the personal spheres of life, such as by affording family members the opportunities that can result from a successful business.

Entrepreneurship does not require workaholism or any other qualities that detract from a healthy and happy personal, familial, and social life. Neither the CEO I nor the CEO II type entrepreneur needs to sacrifice any aspect of his or her human potential. On the contrary, entrepreneurship calls for maximizing resources, and certainly holistic health—involving mind, body, and spirit—is necessary to achieve optimal human resources.

Qualities of the entrepreneur include a host of positive traits: internalization of responsibility, self-confidence, desire to achieve, goal-oriented leadership, objectivity, perceptiveness, adaptability, persistence, tolerance for ambiguity, open-mindedness, flexibility, future orientation, risk taking, and a number of other personal qualities compatible with any humanistic viewpoint. In other words, being an entrepreneur can accommodate a healthy effort to attain self-actualization.

A holistic stance means that the entrepreneur must seek to effectively enhance and integrate his or her mind, body, and spirit. There must be elimination, or least minimization, of adverse body-mind conditions, such as those that might be brought on by stress, "dis-ease," and maladaptive habits. Instead of succumbing to illogical and unhealthy ideas (say, the belief that life is not worth living without wealth, or that work is more important than all else), the holistic entrepreneur applies logic and rational thinking to every decision, thereby protecting his or her own organism. The same sort of self-control and creativity that are applied to work-related decisions should be applied to organism-related decisions about proper diet, exercise, recreation, leisure, physical fitness, weight control, relaxation, and avoidance of maladaptive habits (for example, substance abuse or obsessive-compulsive behavior). Illogical defense mechanisms, which sap away needed energy, should be eliminated. In discussing "overload," Bellak (1975, p. 156) states, "A maximum of defensiveness makes us narrowminded, overly rigid, opinionated, intolerant, and eventually paralyzed." Of these qualities, none fosters productivity, health, or entrepreneurship.

In considering CEO I and CEO II types of entrepreneurs, one may assume that CEO I, with a greater ability to take calculated risks, will more readily set aside the ensured increase in business profits from being on the job in favor of replenishing his or her organism through such off-duty experiences as enjoying family and friends. By investing in holistic health, the entrepreneur is increasing the likelihood that business efforts will bring long-term benefits. Workaholism can lead to short-term rewards but also to disability or illness that eliminates long-term rewards. Pelletier (1977, p. 6) says, "Stress-induced disorders have long since replaced infectious disease as the major medical problem of the post-industrial nations." According to Lowen and Lowen (1977, p. 4), "The more alive one is, the more energy one has and vice versa." The mental health entrepreneur surely cannot have business success without energy and life.

The mental health entrepreneur needs what Rogers (1977, p. 7) calls "person power": "There is in every organism, at whatever level, an underlying flow of movement toward constructive fulfillment of its inherent possibilities." The press toward positive fulfillment of personal potential furthers entrepreneurship and requires elimination of defensive maneuvers and self-defeating behaviors, to allow the mental health entrepreneur to perceive and behave in a positive fashion. Rogers

(1977) believes that person-centered growth occurs when "there is increasing recognition of the importance of feelings, as well as reason, of emotion as well as intellect" (p. 49); the benefits will include "greater mutual trust, personal growth, and shared interest" (p. 50), and "a more realistic appraisal of the needs each [person] can meet in the other" (p. 52).

Effort is required to move toward the fully functioning self. Maslow (1962, p. 36) urges "(a) acceptance and expression of the inner core or self, i.e., actualization of these latent capacities and potentialities, 'full functioning,' availability of human and personal essence; and (b) minimal presence of ill health, neurosis, psychosis, of loss or diminution of the basic human or personal capacities." In other words, the mental health entrepreneur who engages in self-examination can gain a better awareness of his or her own (and others') resources, assets and liabilities, and abilities and limitations.

The mental health entrepreneur is in the process of moving toward a fully functioning state of being (which may be unattainable). Being requires psychological freedom (Rogers, 1961, p. 191), by which a person "is more able to live fully in and with each and all of his feelings and reactions. He makes increasing use of all of his organic equipment to sense, as accurately as possible, the existential situation within and without. He makes use of all of the information his nervous system can thus supply, using it in awareness, but recognizing that his total organism may be, and often is, wiser than his awareness. He is more able to permit his total organism to function freely in all its complexity in selecting, from the multitude of possibilities, the behavior which in this moment of time will be more generally and genuinely satisfying. He is able to put more trust in his organism in this functioning, not because it is infallible, but because he can be fully open to the consequences of each of his actions and correct them if they prove to be less than satisfying."

For mental health entrepreneurship, the payoff is in operating with a healthy personality. As Jourard (1971, p. 28) says, "Healthy personalities play their roles satisfactorily and derive personal satisfaction from role enactment; more, they keep growing and they maintain high-level wellness." Thorne (1965,

p. 15) put it well: "The rewards of life go only to the worthy. Do not expect something for nothing, else you will reap exactly what you sow." Thorne also cautions (p. 155) against unrealistic expectations, impatience, excessive dependence on others, undue rigidity, stubbornness, and failure to plan: "Psychological health, as a whole, depends upon the degree to which any person succeeds in actualizing his potentials in learning to cope with all the standard situations of life, living actively and creatively, and acting out many roles well."

Comments in earlier chapters may have seemed to deride humanistic principles, but those comments were directed at the use of humanistic clinical techniques to the exclusion of more objective, academically based, and change-oriented procedures. Public policy does not currently tolerate humanistic approaches (compare the 1960s or the early 1970s, before society underwent the revolution in consumerism and availability of legal remedies). Humanistic principles are, however, important to human resource development.

For maximum entrepreneurship, the mental health CEO must accept that life is a priceless asset and cultivate an enriching life-style. "So far as motivational status is concerned, healthy people have sufficiently gratified their basic needs for safety, belongingness, love, respect and self-esteem so that they are motivated primarily by trends to self-actualization . . . an unceasing trend toward unity, integration or synergy within the person" (Maslow, 1971, p. 19).

The Entrepreneurial Score

Woody (1984) uses the acronym S-C-O-R-E for five strategies to achieve mental health: S = the self-concept; C = control (or responsibility); O = originality (or creativity); R = relaxation; and E = energy. These strategies have special usefulness for the mental health CEO who wishes to win as an entrepreneur.

Strategy S = The Self. "Person power" depends on self-actualization. To move forward, the entrepreneur must develop self-acceptance, which makes it feasible to gain personal meaning from every experience. In the business context, this will open the door to innovation and daring, but only with analysis and calculation of risk. In dealing with business sources (employees, community referral agents, clients), the mental health entrepreneur should be authentic (present no masks) and transparent (offer willing disclosure), get rid of unhealthy defense mechanisms (accept responsibility for one's self and one's actions), use helpful communications, and bring qualities of trust, caring, and sharing to relationships.

Strategy C = Control. Entrepreneurial leadership cannot prevail without internalization of responsibility. Mental health CEOs must take control of business operations and assume responsibility for the functioning of themselves and others. Granted, each individual in the mental health practice must always have self-determination, but the mental health CEO can exercise appropriate control by monitoring and guiding everyone's perceptions and behaviors, especially as these are manifested in people's work. The locus of control will be internal. In accord with entrepreneurship, the mental health CEO will therefore be capable of action, keenly aware of options, and dedicated to accomplishing personal and business objectives. Internalization of control leads to confidence, competence, and resistance to external control (such as from competing practitioners or from professional associations). Independence does not preclude constructive sharing and dependence, as long as there are contributions to self-actualization, health, and entrepreneurship.

Strategy O = Originality. Originality is in total harmony with entrepreneurship, which requires a creative composition. Creativity can be abstract (an idea or a concept) or concrete (a work of art). Everyone is capable of some form of creativity. Like entrepreneurial ability, creativity does not depend on genetic endowment; it can be learned and cultivated.

Entrepreneurship and creativity may have a shared source: "Creativity is a yearning for immortality. We human beings know that we must die. We have, strangely enough, a word for death. We know that each of us must develop the courage to confront death. Yet we also must rebel and struggle against it. Creativity comes from this struggle—out of the rebellion the creative act is born. Creativity is not merely the innocent spontaneity of our youth and childhood; it must also be married to the passion of the adult human being, which is a passion to live beyond one's death" (May, 1975, p. 27).

Entrepreneurship needs originality, or creativity, to seed, fertilize, and harvest unique achievements, as required for distinguished market positioning. Whether from a psychological or a success orientation, the more creative but logical the venture, the greater the potential reward. In mental health entrepreneurship, originality requires diversification (breaking through cognitive and behavioral restrictions), a touch of daring (willingness to be different), and esthetic experience (enrichment through creation).

Strategy R = Relaxation. To be effective, the mental health CEO cannot be dull. Being on the cutting edge of the profession and the business, he or she must be razor-sharp in every thought and tactic. Relaxation is one of the best whetstones for sharpening one's entrepreneurial blades.

Whatever approach to relaxation one chooses, one needs a quiet environment, the use of a healthful mental device, a passive attitude, and comfort (Benson, 1976). At first glance, it is easy to see how these conditions are almost antithetical to what is encountered in the workaday world. Neither the CEO I nor the CEO II type entrepreneur needs to be a Type A person. Instead, the healthy entrepreneur will cultivate stress-free Type B behavior. This may require deprogramming and reprogramming, as well as a lot of self-disciplined practice at removing oneself from unhealthy business-related conditions. Relaxation promotes a healthy organism, and without health, entrepreneurship is to no avail.

Strategy E = Energy. Energy is a prerequisite of entrepreneurship. The mental health CEO will be the driving force behind the development of the business. Unless he or she is excited by the business prospects and can make rapid executions to fulfill objectives, success will be hampered. Constitutional endowment may bestow potentials and impose restrictions, but energy relies far more on physical and mental conditioning than on heredity. Nutrition and diet, weight control, physical fitness, and adaptive habits contribute to the reserve of energy that the mental health CEO can bring to entrepreneurial efforts. The professional style should preserve the energy supply (eliminate wasted effort), prospect for alternative energy sources (find rewards), and invest in energy stocks (not put too much effort into an activity that may pay no dividends).

Coping with the Changing Demands
of Business and the Profession

The business and professional worlds have a common core: They require change. This never-fixed condition has, of course, been mentioned earlier (such as in the context of never settling on a permanent business plan or marketing mix). In terms of integrating the professional and personal self-concepts, there must be an accommodation of the vicissitudes of business and professionalism. It is impossible to predict every change that will occur in business and professionalism, and success is never ensured in any aspect of mental health practice. The professional-personal self-concept blend should prepare one for ups and downs, and the practitioner should not feel denigration because of inconsistent performance or faltering success. On the contrary, these variances can be viewed as proof of a dynamic quality that is essential to success, and personal fulfillment can be gleaned from knowing that changes signal a potential for future benefits.

A Fulfilling Life-Style

Perhaps it is a major drawback that the mental health CEO will always be left wanting and needing something new and better, but this unending quest does not have to be a negative condition. It can be a framework for health and enjoyment. Looking to the future, the mental health entrepreneur can de-

rive momentum from assessment and appreciation of past accomplishments and current benefits. Human nature leads to the
need to share these positives factors with those one cares for,
whether they are family members, professional associates, or
support staff members. Part of the enriching dimension of
entrepreneurship is passing on benefits to others who have contributed to the enterprise. Such benefits reach all the way to the
larger society.

Entrepreneurship promotes personal and familial fulfillment, but only if the mental health practitioner is able to regulate work-related conditions to avoid an unhealthy life-style. It
is not a contradiction of entrepreneurship to refuse to work;
too much work, in fact, contradicts entrepreneurship. Optimal
entrepreneurship will be supported by the mental health practitioner's defining his or her personal priorities and developing a
life-style that will fulfill them. The old adage "Some people live
to work, and others work to live" can guide the proper balanc-
ing of work effort and personal life-style. Certainly, avoiding
workholism and burnout, in favor of attaining health and happiness, is compatible with a learned definition of business success in mental health practice.

References

Adams, C. F. *Common Sense in Advertising.* New York: McGraw-Hill, 1965.

American Medical Association v. *FTC* (94 F.T.C. 701, final order, Oct. 12, 1979).

American Psychological Association. "Ethical Principles of Psychologists." *American Psychologist,* 1981a, *36* (6), 633–638.

American Psychological Association. "Specialty Guidelines for the Delivery of Services." *American Psychologist,* 1981b, *36* (6), 639–681.

American Psychological Association. "General Guidelines for Providers of Psychological Services." *American Psychologist,* 1987a, *42,* 712–723.

American Psychological Association. "Report of the Ethics Committee: 1986." *American Psychologist,* 1987b, *42* (7), 730–734.

August, J. D., and Bennett, S. A. "Subchapter S Corporations." In Florida Bar Continuing Legal Education Committee (ed.), *Florida Small Business Practice.* Tallahassee: Florida Bar, 1986.

Bales, J. "FTC Demands End to Ad, Fee-Splitting Restrictions." *APA Monitor,* 1988, *19* (3), 19.

Barnes, N. G. "The Consumer Decision Process for Professional Services Marketing: A New Perspective." *Journal of Professional Services Marketing,* 1986, *2* (1/2), 39–45.

Bates v. *State Bar of Arizona* (433 U.S. 350, 1977).

Baty, G. B. *Entrepreneurship for the Eighties.* Reston, Va.: Reston Publishing, 1981.

Bauer, R. A. "Consumer Behavior as Risk Taking." In R. S. Hancock (ed.), *Dynamic Marketing for a Changing World.* Chicago: American Marketing Associates, 1960.

Bell, M. L. *Marketing: Concepts and Strategy.* Boston: Houghton Mifflin, 1972.

Bellak, L. *Overload: The New Human Condition.* New York: Human Sciences Press, 1975.

Benson, H. *The Relaxation Response.* New York: Avon, 1976.

Besharov, D. J. *The Vulnerable Social Worker: Liability for Serving Children and Families.* Silver Springs, Md.: National Association of Social Workers, 1985.

Bion, W. R. *Experience in Groups.* New York: Basic Books, 1961.

Bloom, P. N. *Advertising, Competition, and Public Policy: A Simulation Study.* Cambridge, Mass.: Ballinger, 1976.

Boje, D. M., and Ulrich, D. "The Qualitative Side of Leadership." In R. Tannenbaum, N. Margulies, F. Massarik, and Associates (eds.), *Human Systems Development.* San Francisco: Jossey-Bass, 1985, 302–318.

Bonner, H. *Group Dynamics: Principles and Applications.* New York: Ronald, 1959.

Bradford, D. L., and Cohen, A. R. *Managing for Excellence: The Guide to Developing High Performance in Contemporary Organizations.* New York: Wiley, 1984.

Bradford, W. M., and Davis, G. B. *Personal and Business Tax and Financial Planning for Psychiatrists.* Washington, D.C.: American Psychiatric Press, 1984.

Braun, I. *Building a Successful Professional Practice with Advertising.* New York: AMACOM, 1981.

Brigham, J. C. *Social Psychology.* Boston: Little, Brown, 1986.

Brown, D., Pryzwansky, W. B., and Schulte, A. C. *Psychological Consultation.* Boston: Allyn & Bacon, 1987.

Casson, M. *The Entrepreneur: An Economic Theory.* New York: Barnes & Noble, 1982.

Charles, S. C., Wilbert, J. R., and Kennedy, E. C. "Physicians' Self-Reports of Reactions to Malpractice Litigation." *American Journal of Psychiatry,* 1984, *141,* 563–565.

Clewett, R. H., and Stasch, S. F. *The Product Managers in Consumer Packaged-Goods Industries.* Evanston, Ill.: Graduate School of Management, Northwestern University, 1974.

Cueny, D., Miller, K., and Eldridge, M. K. "The Healthcare Account Executive—A Sales Approach to Healthcare Marketing." *Health Marketing Quarterly,* 1986, *3* (2/3), 85–92.

Cunningham, L. F., and Bennett, R. O. "Systematic Design of Effective Marketing Research Data Requirements in Health Maintenance Organizations." *Health Marketing Quarterly,* 1987, *4* (3/4), 89–105.

Day, G. S., and Wensley, R. "Assessing Advantage: A Framework for Diagnosing Competitive Superiority." *Journal of Marketing,* 1988, *52* (2), 1–20.

Federal Trade Commission. *Federal Trade Commission Decisions,* 1979, *94,* 701–1041.

Felton, A. P. "Making the Marketing Concept Work." *Harvard Business Review,* 1959, *37,* 55–65.

Ficker, V. B. *Effective Supervision.* Westerville, Ohio: Merrill, 1975.

Fisher, K. "Charges Catch Clinicians in Cycle of Shame, Slip-ups." *American Psychological Association Monitor,* 1985, *16* (5), 6–7.

Forman, B. D., and Forman, K. S. *Fundamentals of Marketing the Private Psychotherapy Practice.* Springfield, Ill.: Thomas, 1987.

Goldfarb v. *Virginia State Bar* (421 U.S. 733, 1975).

Goodstein, L. D. "Across My Desk." *American Psychological Association Monitor,* 1986, *17* (3), 3.

Hall, D. T., and Goodale, J. G. *Human Resource Management.* Glenview, Ill.: Scott, Foresman, 1986.

Hartley, S. W., and Lee, P. L. "Implementation of Services Marketing Program: Key Areas for Improvement." *Journal of Professional Services Marketing,* 1986, *2* (1/2), 25–37.

Hill, C. J., and Fannin, W. R. "Professional Service Marketing Strategies for the 80s." *Journal of Professional Services Marketing,* 1986, *2* (1/2), 11–23.

Hill, C. T., and Stull, D. E. "Sex Differences in Effects of Social and Value Similarity in Same-Sex Friendship." *Journal of Social and Personality Psychology,* 1981, *41,* 488–502.

Hogan, D. B. *The Regulation of Psychotherapists.* Vol. 3. *A Review of Malpractice Suits in the United States.* Cambridge, Mass.: Ballinger, 1979.

Hollander, E. P. *Leadership Dynamics: A Practical Guide to Effective Relationships.* New York: Free Press, 1978.

Houston, F. S. "The Marketing Concept: What It Is and What It Is Not." *Journal of Marketing,* 1986, *50* (2), 81–87.

Janis, I. L. *Groupthink: Psychological Studies of Policy Decisions and Fiascoes.* (2nd ed.) Boston: Houghton Mifflin, 1983.

Jourard, S. M. *The Transparent Self.* (Rev. ed.). New York: Van Nostrand Reinhold, 1971.

Kagle, J. D. *Social Work Records.* Homewood, Ill.: Dorsey Press, 1984.

Keeton, W. P., Dobbs, D. B., Keeton, R. E., and Owen, D. G. *Prosser and Keeton on the Law of Torts.* (5th ed.). St. Paul, Minn.: West, 1984.

Kets de Vries, M.F.R., and Miller, D. *The Neurotic Organization: Diagnosing and Changing Counterproductive Styles of Management.* San Francisco: Jossey-Bass, 1984.

Kiesler, C. A., and Sibulkin, A. E. *Mental Hospitalization: Myths and Facts About a National Crisis.* Newbury Park, Calif.: Sage, 1987.

Konopa, L. J., and Calabro, P. J. "Adoption of the Marketing Concept by Large Northeastern Ohio Manufacturers." *Akron Business and Economic Review,* 1971, *2,* 9–13.

Kotler, P. *Principles of Marketing.* Englewood Cliffs, N.J.: Prentice-Hall, 1980.

Kotler, P., and Zaltman, G. "Social Marketing: An Approach to Planned Social Change." *Journal of Marketing,* 1971, *35,* 3–12.

Lewin, K., Lippett, R., and White, R. "Patterns of Aggressive Behavior in Experimentally Created Social Climates." *Journal of Social Psychology,* 1939, *10,* 271–299.

Lowen, A., and Lowen, L. *The Way to Vibrant Health: A Manual of Bioenergetic Exercises.* New York: Harper & Row, 1977.

McCarthy, C. "Lawyer's Effort to Help Not Understood." *American Trial Lawyers Association Advocate,* 1986, *12,* 2.

McCarthy, E. J., and Perreault, W. D., Jr. *Basic Marketing.* (8th ed.). Homewood, Ill.: Irwin, 1984.

McClelland, D. C. *The Achieving Society.* New York: Free Press, 1967.

McDaniel, S. W., Smith, L. M., and Smith, K. T. "The Status of Physician Advertising." *Journal of Professional Services Marketing,* 1986, *2* (1/2), 131–145.

McDonald, C. J. *Action-Oriented Decisions in Ambulatory Medicine.* New York: Year Book, 1981.

McGrath, M. H. "Professional Service Corporations." In Florida Bar Continuing Legal Education Committee (ed.), *Florida Small Business Practice.* Tallahassee: Florida Bar, 1986.

MacStravic, R. S. "Marketing Circles in Practice Development." *Journal of Professional Services Marketing,* 1986, *2* (1/2), 47–54.

Mahon, J. J. *The Marketing of Professional Accounting Services.* New York: Wiley, 1978.

Mangold, W. F., Berl, R., Pol, L., and Abercrombie, C. L. "An Analysis of Consumer Reliance on Personal and Nonpersonal Sources of Professional Service Information." *Journal of Professional Services Marketing,* 1987, *2* (3), 9–29.

Maslow, A. H. "Some Basic Propositions of a Growth and Self-Actualization Psychology." In A. W. Combs (ed.), *Perceiving-Behaving-Becoming: A New Focus for Education.* Washington, D.C.: Association for Supervision and Curriculum Development, 1962.

Maslow, A. H. "Deficiency Motivation and Growth Motivation." In A. R. Mahrer and L. Pearson (eds.), *Creative Developments in Psychotherapy.* Cleveland, Ohio: Case Western Reserve University Press, 1971.

May, R. *The Courage to Create.* New York: Norton, 1975.

Mechanic, D. "Some Dilemmas in Health Care Policy." In J. B. McKinlay (ed.), *Issues in Health Care Policy.* Cambridge, Mass.: MIT Press, 1981.

Meichenbaum, D., and Turk, D. C. *Facilitating Treatment Adherence: A Practitioner's Guidebook.* New York: Plenum, 1987.

Meredith, G. B., Nelson, R. E., and Neck, P. A. *The Practice of Entrepreneurship.* Geneva, Switzerland: International Labour Office, 1982.

Michener, H. A., DeLamater, J. D., and Schwartz, S. H. *Social*

Psychology. San Diego, Calif.: Harcourt Brace Jovanovich, 1986.

Mobley, M. F., Elkins, R. L., and Mobley, M. C. "An Overview of Practical Marketing Considerations for Private Practice Psychiatrists." *Journal of Marketing for Mental Health,* 1987/88, *1* (2), 65–69.

Moldenhauer, C. A. "The Brochure: A Powerful Key to Expanding Your Service." *Journal of Marketing for Mental Health,* 1987/88, *1* (2), 125–133.

Nordstrom, R. D., and Steinke, E. "How Do Patients Select a Doctor?" *Health Marketing Quarterly,* 1987, *4* (3/4), 37–46.

O'Bryan, D. W. "Progress Reports." *Trial,* 1988, *24* (1), 31–32.

Olle, D. J., and Macaulay, R. B. "General Partnerships." In Florida Bar Continuing Legal Education Committee (ed.), *Florida Small Business Practice.* Tallahassee: Florida Bar, 1986.

Overcast, T. D., and Sales, B. D. "Psychological and Multidisciplinary Corporations." *Professional Psychology,* 1981, *12* (6), 749–760.

Overcast, T. D., Sales, B. D., and Pollard, M. R. "Applying Antitrust Laws to the Professions: Implications for Psychology." *American Psychologist,* 1982, *37* (5), 517–525.

Ownby, R. L. *Psychological Reports.* Brandon, Vt.: Clinical Psychology Publishing, 1987.

Parker, C. "A Paradigm Shift in Health Care: Marketing Implications for Physicians in Solo Practice." *Health Marketing Quarterly,* 1987, *4* (3/4), 11–20.

Parsons, R. J., and Tomkinson, R. E., Jr. "Physician Marketing the Quick and Easy Way—Almost." *Health Marketing Quarterly,* 1987, *4* (3/4), 21–26.

Parsons, R. J., Youkstetter, D. F., Burton, D. A., and Willson, W. K. "Effects on Physicians from Changing Megatrends in Health Care." *Health Marketing Quarterly,* 1986, *4* (2), 9–20.

Pelletier, K. R. *Mind as Healer, Mind as Slayer: A Holistic Approach to Preventing Stress Disorders.* New York: Delacorte, 1977.

Peterson, C. M., Forham, S. E., and Jones, R. L. "Self-Management: An Approach to Patients with Insulin-Dependent Diabetes Mellitis." *Diabetes Care,* 1980, *3*, 82–87.

Pinchot, G., III. *Intrapreneuring.* New York: Harper & Row, 1985.

Ray, M. L. *Advertising and Communication Management.* Englewood Cliffs, N.J.: Prentice-Hall, 1982.

Roach, W. J., Jr., Chernoff, S. N., and Esley, C. L. *Medical Records and the Law.* Rockville, Md.: Aspen Systems, 1985.

Rogers, C. R. *On Becoming a Person.* Boston: Houghton Mifflin, 1961.

Rogers, C. R. *Carl Rogers on Personal Power.* New York: Delacorte, 1977.

Rossi, P. H., Wright, J. D., Fisher, G. A., and Willis, G. "The Urban Homeless: Estimating Composition and Size." *Science,* 1987, *235,* 1336–1341.

Rubright, R., and MacDonald, D. *Marketing Health and Human Services.* Rockville, Md.: Aspen Systems, 1981.

Ruekert, R. W., and Walker, O. C., Jr. "Marketing's Interaction with Other Functional Units: A Conceptual Framework and Empirical Evidence." *Journal of Marketing,* 1987, *51* (1), 1–19.

Russ, R. C., Gold, J. A., and Stone, W. F. "Attraction to a Dissimilar Stranger as a Function of Level of Effectance Arousal." *Journal of Experimental Social Psychology,* 1979, *15,* 459–466.

Russ, R. C., Gold, J. A., and Stone, W. F. "Opportunity for Thought as a Mediator of Attraction to a Dissimilar Stranger: A Further Test of an Information-Seeking Interpretation." *Journal of Experimental Social Psychology,* 1980, *16,* 562–572.

Sales, B. D. "The Legal Regulation of Psychology: Scientific and Professional Interactions." In C. J. Scheirer and B. L. Hammonds (eds.), *Psychology and the Law.* Washington, D.C.: American Psychological Association, 1983.

Saywell, R. M., Jr., and McHugh, G. J. "Organization of the Health Care Delivery System in the U.S." In G. T. Troyer and S. L. Salman (eds.), *Handbook of Health Care Risk Management.* Rockville, Md.: Aspen Systems, 1986.

Schollhammer, H., and Kuriloff, A. H. *Entrepreneurship and Small Business Management.* New York: Wiley, 1979.

Shostack, G. L. "Service Positioning Through Structural Change." *Journal of Marketing,* 1987, *51* (1), 34–43.

Spitz, A. E., and Sauber, M. "An Overview of the Business of Genocide in the United States: Who Is Culpable?" *Health Marketing Quarterly,* 1987, *4* (3/4), 119–128.

Stogdill, R. "Personal Factors Associated with Leadership." *Journal of Psychology,* 1948, *25,* 35–71.

Surprenant, C. F., and Solomon, M. R. "Predictability and Personalization in the Service Encounter." *Journal of Marketing,* 1987, *15* (2), 86–96.

Thorne, F. C. *Tutorial Counseling: How to Be Psychologically Healthy.* Brandon, Vt.: Clinical Psychology Publishing, 1965.

Trent, C. L. "Psychiatric Malpractice Insurance and Its Problems: An Overview." In W. E. Barton and C. J. Sanborn (eds.), *Law and the Mental Health Professions.* New York: International Universities Press, 1978.

Turkington, C. "Response to Crisis: Pay Up or Go Naked." *American Psychological Association Monitor,* 1986, *17* (4), 6–7.

Tyler, L. E. *The Work of the Counselor.* (3rd ed.) East Norwalk, Conn.: Appleton-Century-Crofts, 1969.

Tyler, T. R., and Sears, D. O. "Coming to Like Obnoxious People When We Must Live with Them." *Journal of Personality and Social Psychology,* 1977, *35,* 200–211.

Van Doren, D. C., and Relle, P. B. "Confronting Intangibility: A Practical Approach." *Journal of Professional Services Marketing,* 1987, *2* (3), 31–40.

Walker, M. *Advertising and Promoting the Professional Practice.* New York: Hawthorn Books, 1979.

Waters, K. A., and Murphy, G. F. *Medical Records in Health Information.* Rockville, Md.: Aspen Systems, 1979.

Webster, C. "Strategies for Becoming Marketing-Oriented in the Professional Services Arena." *Journal of Professional Services Marketing,* 1987, *2* (4), 11–27.

Wheatley, E. W. "Rainmakers, Mushrooms, and Immaculate Conception: Internal Marketing for Professional Services Firm Associates." *Journal of Professional Services Marketing,* 1987, *2* (4), 73–82.

Winston, W. J. "Psychographic/Life-Style Aspects for Target Marketing." *Health Marketing Quarterly,* 1983/84, *1* (2/3), 19–26.

Winston, W. J. "Crisis Management as a Part of Marketing." *Journal of Professional Services Marketing,* 1986a, *2* (1/2), 7–10.

Winston, W. J. "Need for Competitor Analysis." *Health Marketing Quarterly,* 1986b, *4* (2), 5–7.

Winston, W. J. "Basics of Using Focus Groups." *Health Marketing Quarterly,* 1987, *4* (3/4), 5–9.

Winter, J. P. "Getting Your House in Order with Internal Marketing: A Marketing Prerequisite." *Health Marketing Quarterly,* 1985, *3* (1), 69–77.

Woody, R. H. *Practical Mental Health.* Springfield, Ill.: Thomas, 1984.

Woody, R. H. "Groupthink in the Law Firm." *Michigan Bar Journal,* 1987, *66* (6), 573–576.

Woody, R. H. *Fifty Ways to Avoid Malpractice: A Guidebook for Mental Health Professionals.* Sarasota, Fla.: Professional Resource Exchange, 1988a.

Woody, R. H. *Protecting Your Mental Health Practice: How to Minimize Legal and Financial Risk.* San Francisco: Jossey-Bass, 1988b.

Worchel, S., and Cooper, J. *Understanding Social Psychology.* (3rd ed.). Homewood, Ill.: Dorsey Press, 1983.

Wright, R. H. "What to Do Until the Malpractice Lawyer Comes: A Survivor's Manual." *American Psychologist,* 1981, *36* (12), 1535–1541.

Young, T. J. "Moving Your Office." *Trial,* 1988, *24* (1), 24–28.

Zander, A. *The Purposes of Groups and Organizations.* San Francisco: Jossey-Bass, 1985.

Index

A

Abercrombie, C. L., 55
Accountability, and ethical complaints, 164
Accountants: selecting, 144–146; as tax advisers, 27; teamwork with, 147–148
Accounts: and debt collection, 156–158; and educating client, 148–149; and fee setting, 150–152; and logging services, 152–154; making payments on, 154–156; managing, 148–158; and motivating client payment, 149–150
Adams, C. F., 78–79
Advertising: agents for, 67–68; and business plan, 19; criticisms of, 62, 85. *See also* Promotion
American Association for Marriage and Family Therapy, 38
American Medical Association v. *FTC,* and restraint on advertising, 63
American Psychological Association, 3, 6, 64, 153, 154, 160, 164, 174
Announcements, for promotion, 80–81
Antitrust laws, and marketing, 7, 63
Architects, and office design, 142–143

Attitude-structure analysis, for psychographics, 51–53
Attorney: and debt collection, 157; and risk management, 170, 173; selection of, 146–147, 169; teamwork with, 147–148
Attraction, in practice group, 92–94
Auditor, role of, 145–146
August, J. D., 100

B

Bales, J., 6, 55, 64
Barnes, N. G., 4, 5, 43
Bates v. *State Bar of Arizona,* and association restraint on advertising, 63
Baty, G. B., 14, 18, 23, 49, 144–145, 146, 189–190
Bauer, R. A., 55
Bell, M. L., 48
Bellak, L., 198
Bennett, R. O., 18, 37
Bennett, S. A., 100
Benson, H., 202
Berl, R., 55
Besharov, D. J., 167
Bion, W. R., 117–118
Bloom, P. N., 62, 63, 188
Boje, D. M., 178–179
Bonner, H., 116
Bradford, D. L., 183
Bradford, W. M., 26, 144, 146

215